C000148769

A WHITE KNUCKLE
RIDE THROUGH
LIFE

D H Rockley

Mereo Books

2nd Floor, 6-8 Dyer Street, Cirencester, Gloucestershire, GL7 2PF

An imprint of Memoirs Book Ltd. www.mereobooks.com

A White Knuckle Ride Through Life: 978-1-86151-946-7

First published in Great Britain in 2019 by Mereo Books,
an imprint of Memoirs Books Ltd.

Copyright ©2019

D H Rockley has asserted his right under the Copyright Designs and Patents
Act 1988 to be identified as the author of this work.

A CIP catalogue record for this book is available from the British Library.
This book is sold subject to the condition that it shall not by way of trade
or otherwise be lent, resold, hired out or otherwise circulated without
the publisher's prior consent in any form of binding or cover, other than
that in which it is published and without a similar condition, including this
condition being imposed on the subsequent purchaser.

The address for Memoirs Books Ltd. can be
found at www.memoirspublishing.com

Memoirs Books Ltd. Reg. No. 7834348

Typeset in 11/15pt Century Schoolbook
by Wiltshire Associates Ltd.
Printed and bound in Great Britain

Contents

~~~~

Dedication

~~~

To my family
with love to you all, past and present

Acknowledgment

~~~~~

I got enormous encouragement from my friends, and especially from David Donnison, a Glasgow University emeritus and dear friend of mine who, when he was alive, lived part-time on Easdale Island, where I too lived for many years. Thank you Alison Colin for unwavering support whilst I was building my boat, moving to Scotland and during my yacht chartering adventures. A big thank you to Annabel Gregory for her endless patience and cups of tea as well as for helping me with the manuscript, also to Rosalea Collinge for her editing advice. A big thank you to Antonia Tingle and Chris Newton of Mereo Books for steering me along the thorny path of publishing, to Chris for his words of wisdom, and to their colleague Ray Lipscombe for the lovely cover design. And love to my daughter Corrine, with whom I have shared many of my most cherished memories - thank you Corrine also for one of the cover photos

Introduction

∼∼∼

One night, some friends and I were having a drink in the local pub. The warmth and congeniality of the company prompted us to tell stories, and so, a couple of bottles of good red wine later, we got into telling our real-life stories. When I told them a few of mine, someone said I should write them down, otherwise they could be lost forever.

That got me thinking about how and where I would start. At least a collection of my tales would be something for my family to remember me by. I am not a writer and the last thing I thought I could do was write a book – it takes me all my time to write a letter. Please note, all you wonderful literary critics out there, that this is my first book, it's not a literary masterpiece and was never intended to be, so please be gentle.

I decided not to write about my marital status at different times but stick to my adventures and life stories. It's impossible to remember everything as I never kept a diary, so these memoirs are from memory and may not be quite chronologically correct, apart from sailing, for which I did keep a logbook most of the time.

Chapter 1

Early years

~~~~~~

Hello, my name is Dave Rockley. I was born in the village of Arnold, Nottinghamshire, in 1938 and I'm the youngest of eleven children – seven sisters, three brothers and me. When I was born, the midwife said to my mother, "This one's like a skinned rabbit, Emma, and he's not even breathing". Then after a good slapping, she added, "Don't you think you've got enough children now, Emma?"

I was put into an old white enamel bowl with a chipped blue border round it and left for dead, or so I've been told. My grandmother picked me up, wrapped me in a towel and held me close to her breast. "Oh, my goodness!" she gasped, "He's started breathing!" I don't know if it was the cold bowl that started me breathing or my grandmother picking me up or what, but I must have been very thankful, even though I can't remember it.

One of my first memories was during the war, when I was about two or three years old. Every time the air raid siren sounded, my dad doused the kitchen fire, picked up the big, black cast iron kettle full of simmering hot water from the hob and herded us all down into the cellar. Well, he had to have his cup of tea, no matter what.

The cellar had three open compartments, all smelling damp, with well-worn stone-slabbed floors covered by rugs my mum had made from old clothing, cut into strips and knotted together through a thick sacking base. A game my sisters used to play was trying to spot whose jumper or cardigan was part of the rug, but they worked well at insulating the cold stone floor.

The walls were damp and whitewashed, and in the corners were cobwebs that were thickly decorated with coal dust. One of the end compartments was full of coal and had an outside grate into which the coal was barrowed and poured about once every three months. The middle compartment and the largest were our living quarters during air raids. The beds were bunks made of wood, and my mum tried her best to make it as comfortable and cosy as possible. The whole family weren't there, as it would have been impossible to have them all down in the cellar at the same time. The older ones were either in the armed forces or married and living elsewhere.

The third housed the gas meter, sacks of potatoes, general storage and a whole pig hanging from a hook in the ceiling – well, two halves wrapped in muslin cloth, treated with saltpetre (potassium nitrate) to preserve it.

All the compartments were open to each other via a corridor, and I remember hearing whistling bombs and anti-aircraft guns cracking throughout the night. Often you could hear an explosion and feel a deep vibration, and if there was any liquid in cups or bowls you would see the surface rippling. My dad would say "If you can hear them whistling, they are not for us."

Next day my brother Rex would go outside and collect shrapnel off the streets from the air raids and return with a shoebox full of distorted metal scraps. We all had gas masks which hung in the hallway ready for use. When I was a baby, I had a whole-body gas chamber, but I screamed like hell whenever I was put in it. The family came to the conclusion that they would sooner be gassed than hear that bloody racket, so it was shelved. It was quite a well-engineered piece of kit, I remember seeing it in later years; it had input and output flap valves and crystal filters on the outside, but for a young child it was kind of scary.

My mother kept the cellar very well stocked and equipped, and everything that could be bottled and preserved was down there. Shelves with rows of Kilner jars occupied an entire wall, but the bread dough was left upstairs, rising on the warm hob.

After the all-clear was sounded, my dad would take me

on his shoulders up to the attic window on the third floor to see the extent of the damage. It was an old Victorian three-storey house plus a cellar, and the attic window overlooked the surrounding rooftops, so you could see for miles. If it was a cloudy night, the entire vista was blood red. I remember seeing flames shooting high into the sky from a factory called Jacobies, which had just been hit. It wasn't certain what they were making in this factory, but it must have been something for the war effort as it had been singled out from lots of other factories. It was said at the time that the factory wasn't hit by the air raid but was sabotaged for some reason or other. In the far distance searchlights were still scouring the skies for enemy planes and possible parachutists.

Outside we had a large garden and a well-stocked chicken coop full of Rhode Island Red chickens. My dad grew all our own vegetables, so we were pretty well off foodwise. If we were poor, we certainly never knew it.

The open fields surrounding the village of Arnold were dotted with rows of old cars placed in a line in an attempt to prevent enemy planes or gliders from landing in any open spaces. The cars were there for most of my childhood until well into my teens, and I remember helping my brother strip out the copper brake pipes from them.

One day a couple of men turned up in the street with a horse and cart and started cutting the iron railings that were set in the sandstone-dressed capping of the wall outside the house; all the houses on our side of the street had iron railings. They took the gates and all the railings from the whole street, burning them off with an acetylene torch and leaving just a stub and the lead in which they had been set. I remember gathering the little steel balls that the cutting process had left when it melted the iron. Nobody could do anything about it as it was for the war effort, and I learned later it happened throughout the country.

As I grew up the novelty of kids had somewhat worn off in such a large family, and my sisters began to play a large part in my upbringing. They had an obsession about my neck! They just had to scrub it, almost as if they had a sadistic streak. I would get my revenge by going to the bathroom just as they wanted to get ready to go out on a date.

We had a great upbringing, with lots of fun. Scrumping apples and pears was one of our activities. Getting them into the house was a great problem, but we got around that by being just a little bit late for going in (my parents were strict). The girls would put the apples in their knickers and follow me indoors. I got a clip round the ear and told to "geddup them stairs", while the gals just got ordered straight upstairs. The apples were actually quite nice, considering what they had been through.

Just down the road was a brewery making beer, ales and soft drinks, a huge complex which supplied most of Nottinghamshire's pubs. In its grounds was a large multi-storey building, its walls being mostly glass set in iron frames designed for maximum light input. It was the home of the Apollo soft drinks section of the brewery and was now a temporary barracks for the American Army. We would shout up at the open windows, "Have ya got any gum chum?" and they would throw down a handful of beautifully-wrapped strips of spearmint gum, the like of which we had never seen.

The first soldiers to occupy the building were white, but after a few weeks they were replaced by black soldiers. All of them were very friendly and good to us. We had never seen a black person before, and their shiny black faces and white teeth fascinated us, but we still got chewing gum and candy. I think white and black forces were segregated in those days but I'm not sure.

We played lots of games in the street, like hopscotch, tin-a-lurki and 'farmer, farmer may I cross your golden field', to which the answer was 'Not unless you're wearing pink' or whatever colour the person in the middle of the road would designate, the road being the field.

I slept in the attic with my brother Rex and sometimes Joe, or both, and was always crammed in the middle of the bed gasping for air. It was worse if they had been out on the town and eaten some of that foreign curry stuff, or God knows what else, because then I would get the stink from both ends. Sometimes I was awakened by something hard sticking in my back and an arm was flung around me and I would hear sleeptalking in my ear. "Gerroff!" I would say.

One of the highlights of my childhood was going to the seaside. We would take the train to Skegness. We loved the sea air, the shrill scream of the sea gulls, the candyfloss, the fish and chips, the penny roll machines. I would spend hours looking into the pools at the bottom of the pier supports that the tide had gouged out on its retreat, watching small crabs scurrying about. When the tide was out it would seem to go over the horizon, as the beaches were enormous.

We once stayed at a house called Bleak House which stood all alone in a field and certainly lived up to its name, because it never stopped raining and the wind cut us in half. There was a tidal stream at the bottom of the garden and because the land throughout the area was so flat, when the tide came in small flatfish would swim up it, dabs they are called. I often hooked them, but I never actually landed any unfortunately. The sea was about a mile away from the house but I could smell it, so now, whenever I smell the sea, it takes me back to my early days in Skegness.

Back home my dad would take us out on picnics, which meant walking for miles with him pushing an old handmade wooden wheelbarrow with big recycled pedigree pram wheels fixed to it. Everything we could possibly need was in that barrow, even a bat and ball for playing rounders. He had an uncanny gift of being able to sniff out a pheasant's nest, from twelve to fourteen eggs, and he could tell if they were all right to eat. They were the tastiest little eggs you could get.

Once I was exploring some woodlands with a mate, looking for a special pear tree that we knew was growing near a railway tunnel smoke chimney. When steam trains went through a tunnel those chimneys would allow the white steam and smoke to escape. I think the land must have been part of a garden with an orchard at some time. They were lovely sweet little pears, so we filled our pockets to the brim with them.

On our way home we crossed an open field we had not been in before, so we followed close to a tall red brick-built wall covered in moss and ivy, the border of some big house or farm. I was leading the way and came upon a slight mound covered with earth and patchy grass. I thought nothing of it so I walked over it to pass a thick bed of nettles when suddenly the ground gave way. I sank up to my knees and there was an unimaginable stink which took my breath away. I had fallen into the rib cage of a dead, decomposing cow or horse which had been covered over with soil for quite a long time, making it a shallow grave.

I just stood up to my knees, wondering how I was going to get out without touching it with my hands. I had gone through the ribs and they were catching my pants and stopping me from lifting my legs, and I had visions of wallowing in it as I was trying to get out. Shuffling my feet was just stirring up the stink. I managed to free my pants, but I was heaving uncontrollably. My mate didn't want to come near me and was looking for a stick so he could stay further away from me. I was yelling at him, so he came and with a steadying hand from him I was able to climb out.

"Bloody hell, I can't go home like this" I said, pointing to my pants.

"There's a stream down there" my mate said, "Let's go, I'm going to be sick again".

I stripped off my pants, washed them and bashed them on some stones, then did the same to my plimsolls and socks. It may have been my imagination, but I could smell that stink for days after.

My dad worked for a coal mine. I don't think he was actually down the mine, but he got free coal delivered to our house every three months as a concession. It was just dumped outside in the road by lorry, leaving it to us to barrow it in and pour it into the cellar through a cast iron grate. One enterprising neighbour, a retired schoolteacher who lived near the top of the street, would nonchalantly walk past the heap and selectively pick and then kick a large lump of coal all the way to his house, and he would do this three or four times a day. He must have thought that if he didn't pick it up it wasn't stealing, but my dad caught him in the act one day and said, "If you kick any more of my coal away, I'm going do some kicking with my hobnail boot right up your arse". We never saw him again. The sad part was, if he had asked for some coal my Dad would have taken a barrow load to his house for him – he was that sort of person.

I was ten when my dad died. He was on his way to work on what was called Colliers' Path, a private road leading to Bestwood coal mine. The path wandered its way through a beautiful woodland to the pit where he worked. He suffered a coronary thrombosis and rolled off his bike into a ditch, where he died. His mate found him there and alerted the authorities. The first I knew about it was being awoken by the sound of my mother's crying coming up from downstairs. They kept my dad in the front room for a short time so all the family could have their own little chat to him. It was a very sad time for all of us.

Years later my mum married again. He was a man from Lancashire, who did his best to look after things and we quite liked him, but of course he could never replace my dad. He had bulbous knuckles on both his hands and elbows from arthritis, so he was in pain most of the time but went to work every day. When he died, I think it was from hard work, not old age or health problems.

Chapter 2

The world of work

~~~~~

My first job after leaving school at fifteen was in a stocking-making factory called Morley's, which later became Viyella, and my pay was twenty-two shillings a week, or £1.10p. I was the oil rag at the beck and call of all the knitters, men who worked on the massive machines, which I'm sure must have been a quarter of a mile long. You couldn't see the far end of those machines, which seemed to disappear away into a distant mist, and one knitter had a bike to get from one end to the other. Mind you, everything looks big when you're young.

The really big machines were making the very latest highly fashionable 15-denier nylon stockings with black seams and fancy black heels. The yarn was so fine it had to be stored in a special fog room, where there was a constant pea-souper, and kept at a certain temperature with very high humidity. My biggest dread was when I had to go into the over-locking room to take boxes of stocking blanks to the machinists and generally fetch and carry, and that's when I had to run the gauntlet, so to speak. It was a massive area packed with women of all ages sitting at individual machine tables with bright fluorescent lights hanging just over their heads. I could see the microscopic dust particles rising up from their work into the light, and the first thing I noticed was the warm, strong smells of cheap perfume mixed with body odour, also hot oil from the machines that were constantly working, which hit me as I entered. They were cutting and shaping the stockings with over-locking machines, and the constant clicking and chattering of their activities filled the room.

The women were on piecework, a system where the more you do the more you get paid for. These gals were really hard working and had little or no break, just constant work, so whatever minor entertainment came their way was very welcome indeed to them. As soon as they saw my embarrassed red face that was it, and the redder my face got the better they liked it. The noise and dust were horrendous, and together with the highly-polished jet-black bitumen type floor covered with scraps of thread, dust and nylon stocking material scraps, they made walking through the room quickly quite impossible. Each step had to be carefully placed, especially when I was carrying boxes.

On one occasion I forgot about taking the usual precautions and paid for it with a spectacular skid across the room on my bum, landing under the desk of a machinist. Her legs were wide apart and I was treated to a clear view of black curly hairs spilling out either side of her white knickers. I would have had a face full, had the machine foot pedal not stopped me. I can still see it; she never blinked an eyelid, she was so intent on her work.

I jumped up quick and hit my head on the underside of her table, and all she said was "Careful now". I could feel my face glowing as red as a beetroot, and there were catcalls, whistling and shouts of "Come 'ere me duck" and "Gi's a kiss luv." In those days it was frightening and embarrassing, but at my age it would be exciting and most welcome.

I skied my way back to the door, vowing never to get married and never to go with women, but at just turned fifteen what would you expect in such an atmosphere?

The factory was so big that it was easy to get lost. It occupied both sides of the road and corridors went off into the distance. One corridor was a covered bridge over the road to the other factory, but I soon got to know the ins and outs. I spent a lot of time playing draughts with the stockroom man called Tom. He beat me every time, but eventually he did tell me his technique, so I was able to give him a good run for his money, although I never did beat him.

One evening after work, I was on my way home. It had

been a blistering hot day, so hot it had melted the road tar. I was on my old bike, one I had made from parts of other old bikes I had got from the scrapyard, and the tyres made a swishing, tearing noise on the soft tarmac. I thought it sounded great, so as I was about to pass a large bus queue of young girls on their way home, I stood up to pedal, swinging the bike from side to side, which at speed made the tyres make a loud buzzing noise. The girls could not help but notice me, I thought. But as I passed the end of the queue my bike chain broke and I came off – though not before crushing my testicles on the bike crossbar.

Picking myself up, I looked back at the bus queue but could not see any faces, just watery white blobs. The rear of the queue had swung out into the road to get a better look. Only with a teenager's pride can you do what I did. I picked up the bike as if this had all been deliberate, wheeled it into a convenient covered entrance, grabbed my balls, fell on my knees, rolled into a ball and groaned in pain.

The most embarrassing occurrence of my life took place at that factory. One day I bought a new pair of trousers. I suppose they were the nearest thing you could get to a good pair of jeans as we know them today, AND they had a new-fangled zipper fly fastening instead of the usual buttons, a shining brass metal one.

"Just in from America" the bloke said, holding up a pair with great pride.

"I'd better have 'em then" I said.

I tried them on, and I must say they looked fantastic. I

walked the corridors quite often in my new pants in the hope of seeing the new female medical orderly who worked in a treatment centre on the ground floor, which was just for minor cuts and grazes. I had a wild sort of crush on her but of course she must have been in her mid-twenties and anyway why would she look at me, a fetcher and carrier boy? But she was really beautiful with long auburn hair, a beautiful trim figure and a lovely smiling face.

I was in a bit of a rush one day and zipped up my new flies without taking the usual care to tidy things up. You see we never wore underpants in those days, as it was thought to be sissy or pansy – men didn't wear knickers, that's what girls wore. I trapped my skin in the zip and was in agony, and it was well and truly jammed solid. If you have ever done this, you will know the pain. I had to get down to old Tom, thinking he would know what to do, so I carried some boxes in front of me and tried to walk with my legs open but straight.

Tom studied the problem for a minute and walked off, saying over his shoulder "You should go to the medical centre you know."

"Are you kidding?" I shouted after him "I blush just passing her."

Tom returned with a pair of rusty old pliers.

"What the bloody hell you going to do with them?" I cried out.

"Well I was just…"

I cut him short. "No you're bloody not, it's not a tooth

you know!" I said. But it was inevitable I had to go. The pain was too great and riding my bike home would be impossible.

I walked into the waiting room and announced myself to a pair of thick black-rimmed spectacles and a nose peering over a partition. "Sit down" said the nose. *That's easier said than done*, I thought.

My beautiful medical orderly suddenly appeared at an open door and beckoned me in with a wave and a smile. I walked in the best I could and tried to explain, standing there red-faced with my hands clasped in front of me, but all that came out was gibberish.

"Sit down" she said. I sort of sat down with my legs straight, and she gave me a quizzical look and came over to me. I reluctantly removed my hands, and she came close and bent down

"Oh yes, I can see what the problem is," she said.

I could smell her hair, and the female pheromones that oozed from her. *Oh shit*, I thought, *hope I don't get horny, I must think of something really nasty, quick.* If that happened it would just about kill me in more ways than one.

She studied it for a moment, dabbed something cold on it, gave a little twitch of her wrist and that was it. Well, that's what it seemed like to me as I couldn't see exactly what she was doing, nor did I want to.

"Now try not to do it again, and I suggest you wear underwear, young man," she said.

I flew out, wondering how many times she had done

that, and went right off her. I also wondered how many more zippered flies were about. It was just as well because I never saw her again; I think she must have gone to work elsewhere. I vowed there and then to always wear underpants and didn't care if it was a pansy thing to do. Such was my ordeal.

I had overcome a really major embarrassment and felt suddenly charged with confidence and a dash of adrenalin, having gone through such an ordeal. I even managed to walk through the over-lock machine room with an air of confidence and without going red. Everyone looked up, but no one said anything, which was quite sad because I was ready for them this time.

The turning point had now come for this place, and I decided I had to get out of there while I still had my full complement. My employment at this factory had lasted over a year, but now it was time to think again.

A mate told me he was getting three pounds a week in an engineering factory called Newton and Pycroft near the city centre of Nottingham, making parts for lace machines. They wanted more workers and full training was given, so I went with him to meet the boss. I started work there and then, sitting at a bench filing the rough edges off the thread carrier parts of a lace machine. It was like stepping back into the Victorian age, all overhead belt-driven lathes, grinders, drills, milling machines, the lot, all working from one power source, a massive DC motor. The boss sat all day in an elevated fully-windowed room where he could see everything that was going on, and whenever you looked up, he was watching you. A bright circular light hanging just above his completely bald head made him look like he was wearing a saint's shiny halo.

They had the old butty system in place where you work under a head man, the boss pays him and he pays the gang of workers under him. It sounds daft but it worked. If you cut your finger or whatever, you had to go to Percy the boss in the glass house as we called it, and with great ceremony he would treat it with cotton wool drenched in TCP, which was all he had in the biggest first aid cabinet I'd ever seen, a dozen bottles of the stuff, just TCP.

"Mr Percy, I've cut my thumb."

"Put some of this on it, lad, and it'll be gone in t' morning."

"What, my thumb?"

"Don't be bloody cheeky lad, or I'll swell yer bloody ear!"

Although we made all these components for the lace machines, none of us had ever seen a lace machine until the day they took us to see one that had been assembled in a nearby factory using some of the parts we had made. It really was amazing and wouldn't have looked out of place in a sci-fi film. The detail and workmanship were impeccable. You would have to be some kind of lunatic to have invented a machine like that.

My job here was very repetitive and boring. All there was to look forward to was playing three-card brag at lunch break, and I wasn't much good at that either, so once again it was time to move on. In those days just after the war there was so much work about you could just go from one job to another – being out of work was unheard of.

For the massive sum of three pounds, my brother Rex bought a scrap car. It was a 1936 Morris Eight four-door saloon and there was a lot of work to do on it, but he said he would give it to me for my birthday once we had fixed it. We repaired the car from second-hand parts from the local scrapyards. Some of the bodywork was repaired using papier mâché. The gearbox hadn't any synchromesh, so to change gear we had to double declutch. This meant we depressed the clutch, put the gearstick in neutral, let the clutch out, depressed the clutch again, put the gearstick in the selected gear and released the clutch. It sounds a lot to do just to change gear, it was surprising how quickly we could do it with practice.

The first time we took it out for a spin, we got halfway up a hill and the prop shaft sheared off at the fibre connection just before the gearbox. It ripped out the hydraulic brake pipes and handbrake cable and then hung down on the road, making a fearsome noise. We started rolling downhill backwards, completely out of control. Rex and I jumped out and tried to hold the car back, as it was heading backwards straight for a brand-new Jaguar. The owner was polishing it when he looked up to see us running backwards trying to stop the car as it bore down on him. He started desperately trying to push his car back into his drive. Unfortunately our car was picking up speed, but Rex managed to steer it into a roadside tree, just missing the Jag. The owner breathed a sigh of relief and said he couldn't start his car in time because he had left the keys in the house. We had to push the car into a sports field entrance so we could get it drivable again, but it had to be towed back to our street for us to work on it.

I was walking past a car dealer's place one day when I saw a car that looked fantastic. I can't remember exactly what make or model it was, but it looked a bit like a Ford Zephyr, with lots of chrome all over it, bumpers, trim, and headlights, and it was very cheap. As I was looking at it a chap came out of a small wooden shed and asked if I was interested in the car. "Yes" I said, "but I won't have the money for about a fortnight."

"Well, if you can put a small deposit on it, I'll save it for you," he said. I agreed, and then I asked him if I could come and clean it ready for when I paid for it. "Of course you can lad," he said.

I spent most of my spare time there cleaning and polishing that car, and it looked immaculate. Two or three days before I was to pay for it and while I was doing the finishing touches, the salesman came up to me and said "Sorry lad, here's your deposit back, I can't sell it to you."

"Why?"

"Because I've had an engineer look at it and he has condemned it, sorry lad."

"But I've put all this work into it!"

"I know lad, what a shame," he said, running his hand along the entire length of the car in an admiring gesture on his way back to his little shed.

I was flabbergasted and walked away in a sort of surreal dream; I was too shocked to be angry. A week later I saw the very same car parked outside a grocery shop. I had sussed his greedy little scam, another lesson learnt. I put it behind me and moved on, which was just as well, as I eventually got the car Rex had promised me for my birthday. In those days there was petrol rationing in force, which meant you were only allowed to buy a certain amount of petrol with a coupon from a book you were issued with when you registered your car. You could also drive as a learner without a qualified driver in the car. I could never understand the logic in that, but it's true.

We're now in the mid-1950s, and I was around the age of seventeen or so. These were the rock-n-roll years. A mate and I thought it would be a good idea to get a teddy boy outfit, but you couldn't buy them off the peg – they had to be specially made – so we asked around at various tailors in the city and were told to contact a guy called Tony. We were given his card and went to his address to meet him. He was a great guy and seemed to know exactly what we wanted, and he said we could pay him back in weekly instalments.

Tony was about five years older than us and he certainly had his head screwed on businesswise, because the jackets cost eighty pounds each, a small fortune. He measured us up and we had to have two fittings to make sure they fitted just right. The material was a kind of gabardine cloth, bright red with black velvet lapels and black velvet pocket flaps, green tapered trousers, a shoelace tie and oxblood-stained shoes with thick crepe soles – 'brothel creepers' they were called. I tapered my own trousers, and my mate's, on my mum's old Singer sewing machine. Word got about and I did other guys' pants as well, for a few shillings. We would go to the Palais de Dance Ballroom in Nottingham City and practise jiving, although it was looked down on and we were ordered off the dance floor. We were fans of Bill Haley and the Comets, world famous for *Rock Around the Clock*.

Chapter 3

Down the mine

~~~~~

A short time after leaving my last job, I attended an interview at a colliery which had turned part of its workings into a training facility for young potential miners. It was a pit called Bestwood Colliery, and was where my dad used to work. The pay for just training was about £12 a week, which was big money for me, so I signed on. We spent several weeks in a classroom going though all aspects of mining and safety procedures, including the use of Davy lamps and canaries for gas detection. Smuggling matches, lighters, or cigarettes down the mine was a very serious offence – 'contraband' they called it – and you could be searched at any time. The course was comprehensive and quite enjoyable.

Eventually the big day came when we got to go down into an actual working mine. There were seven of us, plus an old retired miner who was put in charge of our underground activities. He chewed thick black tobacco all the time and could spit the juice great distances with remarkable accuracy. He must have been spitting like this for years, because he had developed special muscles in his cheeks which became quite prominent when he was about to spit juice. His cheeks distorted into a kind of knot on each cheek, exaggerated by having very few teeth, and there was a permanent brown stain down his chin from constant tobacco drizzle. He was a great guy and I give him credit for being able to keep our lot under control in such a small space.

We had to get into a wire cage, where I could see the many layers of rock through the thick wire mesh of what looked for all the world like a prison cell. Being dropped at great speed into a pitch-black hole was very daunting, and not at all good for my bowels. My stomach was left behind at the surface. In an ordinary lift, you don't feel the air rushing past at breath-taking speed or notice layers of smells as you pass through them. At the pit bottom the first thing I noticed was the smell of human sweat, animal shit and other hard-to-recognise smells, along with something like hot, oily, machinery and of course dust, which has its own particular smell, with a touch of pine resin thrown in.

We were shunted away from the main workings of the colliery and into a special area which was a good mock-up of the real thing. There was part of a coalface, pit ponies, wooden props, wagons, just about everything you would be likely to come across in a real mine environment, but there was a lot missing, as I found out later.

We learnt about setting roof props and the use of a Silvester, a kind of ratcheted pulley device for moving great weights. We also learned how to prop up a coalface and the handling of bad-tempered pit ponies, but of course you couldn't blame them for being so nasty, being totally out of their natural environment. One of them bit me on the chest for no apparent reason and I can tell you it was very painful; it wasn't so much a bite as a nasty suck.

The course lasted about eight weeks and most of us became qualified coal miners, with certificates to prove it. All the guys went off to their local mines, and I started work at Gedling Colliery in Nottinghamshire. I was shown around and given a numbered peg fixed to a rail which had a rope hanging from a very high ceiling, at least twenty feet up. The idea was that you hooked your work clothes on it and pulled them up, where they would dry. When you came to work you pulled the rope down, put on your working gear and pulled your clean gear up, which meant you always had dry clothes; crude, but it worked.

The shower room next door was just one long, narrow room with showerheads protruding from the wall about every three feet. While I was training, I never used the showers – the excuse was I didn't get dirty enough, the truth was that I was shy. When I started work proper, it was necessary to shower as I was black with coal dust and decorated with streaks of dried sweat. My first shower there was a bit of an eye opener. I walked in, trying to hide myself with a towel. Rows of men of all shapes and sizes, some built like donkeys, some with little fat buds and some with, well very little. A few men wore a towel all the time in the shower and I thought that could be a good idea. I didn't feel so shy after the first shower and it all became part of the routine.

For a couple of weeks I worked with a team of gate men, whose job was to advance the main gate (tunnel) which supplied the coalface. The man in charge of this trio was a complete control freak who did not like me, for some reason known only to himself. The other two guys were great, although they only seemed to speak or acknowledge me when he was out of earshot. He was a mountain of a man and he treated me with utter contempt. I was supposed to be under his instruction, but he expected me to know what to do and would shout and swear at whatever I did. He called me 'yoth', a corruption of youth, and the other guys would roll their eyes in disgust at his behaviour. He had a very serious youth hate disorder. For all his ranting and raving this man really did know his job, and his tunnelling was as straight as a Roman road. I must say I learnt a lot from this team, but it wasn't easy.

When we were working on a particularly high tunnel which was going up a slight hill, one of the guys got up on some scaffold to chop out the rock so the half circle steel supports could be fitted. He suddenly came over dizzy and fell down, breaking his ankle. It was most likely methane gas, as this is lighter than air and very volatile, so we called in the experts to sort it out. Another gas we came across was black damp. This gas is heavier than air and would settle in low-lying areas such as a dip in the road and act just like water. Both have different characteristics, but both are asphyxiating agents. I stayed with this team and it hardened me up for the tasks ahead. They were a hardy lot and not noted for taking prisoners.

There were air lock doors down the mine which separated the air coming into the mine from the exhaust air going out. When I went through these doors my ears would pop with the sudden change of pressure. In the intake side the air was quite cold and fresh, but the outgoing air was hot, humid and full of smells. There were no toilets down the mine, so I'll leave that to your imagination.

The next stage of my training came as a bit of a shock. I had to work a week or two on what was supposed to be a productive training coal face, C14 it was called. It was a place I will never forget, and I thought it was going to be my grave. Getting onto this face was a complete nightmare. I was told to walk along the main gateway, which was a tunnel, and there was plenty of headroom until I came to the end of it. At first it looked like there was nothing there but a gang of tailgate men working, thanks to the scanty instructions I was given. "I'm looking for C14" I said to a man who I thought was the boss of the gang. "Yes, lad, and you have found it" he said mockingly but smiling. I looked around and said "Well where is it?"

"It's down there, lad" he said pointing to a hole shaped like an elongated letterbox.

"Is that where I'm supposed to go?" I said, bending down to get a better look.

"Yes, me duck, that's it in there."

I had to get down on my belly and pull myself forward on my hands and knees into what looked like the entrance to hell, pushing a pick shovel and seven-pound hammer in front of me. If I'd suffered from claustrophobia this would have been my ultimate nightmare. The wooden pine props were about twenty inches high and a foot across. As I passed them, they cracked, split and oozed resin. I very nearly shat myself with fear. How on earth could anyone visit, let alone work in, a hellhole like this?

Just as I was about to crawl back, thinking I must have got the wrong place, I saw a flash of light, so I headed towards it. Suddenly I was in a much higher space, well two foot six inches to be exact. The light came towards me and said "Hay'up yoth. Yo'll be woking wi' me. I'm Jack, I'll look after ya." He showed me what to do. "Now tek ya pick and chop away at them there gummings and get raight under them coals. I'll come back and see how yo's gerrin' on."

This experienced miner couldn't spend much time talking, as he had to get his nine yards of coal down and onto the conveyor belt. I chopped away at the four-inch-thick grey seam at the very bottom of the coal face. This was where the coal cutter had cut under the coal face, about a yard under, and the debris from the cutter had been compressed by the weight of the coal. The idea was to chop this out so the coal could fall.

I was getting on very well and cleared out about two yards when my training came back to me. I was just thinking I'd better get a couple of props up against the coal face when down it came and rolled on to me, pinning me flat on my back with my legs underneath. My helmet and headlight went flying. I couldn't move or see anything, and the blackness was so intense it almost had a heaviness about it. I could hear Jack shouting "Yo all right yoth?" Thank God the coal broke up as it fell, otherwise there would have been some broken bones.

When there's a fall like this it causes a rush of air along the coalface, and Jack must have felt it. I could see his light dancing from side to side as he scampered on his knees towards me. He rolled the coals off my legs, which were bent under me. I was so shocked by this I didn't acknowledge Jack asking if I was all right. I sat up with his light in my eyes. He slapped my face "Why dint yo answer me?" he yelled. "Ya silly bugger!" I got off light with only a few cuts and bruises, although the cuts had coal embedded in them and it's still there to this day.

Jack and I got on very well after that. My training yardage was three yards and when I'd got that off, I helped him get his nine yards onto the conveyer belt. The whole idea is to pick out the gummings from under the coal for about a yard, then put in a prop to hold back the coal. When you have about nine props the shotfirer drills a hole every so often and fills them with explosive. Then he connects all the wires together and detonates them, which breaks up the coal, and it's up to the miner to get it all onto the conveyer belt. We did get the coal away well before the end of the shift, so we had time to sit and chat, but this wasn't to last as it didn't go unnoticed. I was 'put on the market', which meant I was sent to clear up stints, where miners had not finished their full nine yards. The coalface must be clear along its full length so the cutter can do its thing. Being on the market meant not having a regular workplace where I could store my tools so I had to cart them about from job to job, very often miles away. I could be sent anywhere in the pit.

This was good, as I soon became capable of handling bigger and bigger coal yardages. Because I was young and fit the chargehand tended to give me the worst jobs, or that's what it seemed like to me, but then someone had to do it, so thinking like that made me feel better and not victimised.

I remember being sent to a place where the coal cutter ended its run and started another run in the opposite direction. This meant there were two or more amounts of cutter waste piled up in one stint, so the ground-up rock was right up to the ceiling. It took me two thirds of my shift just to get up to the coalface, and you don't get paid for shifting cutter waste. I must have shovelled six tons of gummings and I was unable to finish my stint.

The next day it was mentioned by the chargehand that I had not completed my stint. I got halfway through telling him the reason why, but he had already turned his attention to someone else. He must have known why.

Eventually I did get my own stint, and soon I was looking and sounding like a proper coal miner. The arse of my pants was worn out from constant rubbing on the heels of my boots in a kneeling position, I swore a lot more, there were no buttons on my shirt, I had worn-out knee pads, a battered old snap tin (lunch box) and was as fit as a butcher's dog. On top of all that I was earning thirty pounds plus a week. I gave my mother fifteen and the other fifteen I spent on booze, girls and other things. This was an absolute fortune in those days, but Wednesday I was borrowing back from my mum. We worked hard and we played even harder. If we were in town, we would visit all the pubs and finish up having a slap-up meal, usually a mixed grill at a Greek restaurant in Nottingham.

There was a fantastic new coal cutter installed and working in the mine, called a trepanner. This was a machine which cut the coal underneath as well as behind and loaded it straight onto the conveyer, which made the miner redundant, or so it was thought. It was in its testing out period, there were no gummings to dig out and the whole operation was semi-automatic. On this coalface the conveyer was a long semi-flexible metal tray with steel rectangular bars running along its length driven by chains either side, a bit like a flexible ladder inside a trough.

Hydraulic rams pushed the conveyer pan to the coalface, just like an escalator but running along the ground. The deputy chargehand was looking for two men to clean up the spilled coal from the side of the trepanner so the metal conveyer could automatically and hydraulically move up to the coalface ready for a return cut. This was a very dangerous job, so it commanded much higher pay.

I volunteered for the job and so did another guy about the same age as me whose name was Mitch, and we immediately got on very well. I borrowed a shovel from the chargehand as my tools were miles away. We got onto this small electric train which pulled about six heavy metal wagons (any electric motors down the pit were encased in heavy cast steel housings and classed as spark-proof for safety reasons) and off we went.

The entrance to the face was via a three-foot square hole which you had to crawl through to get into the stable, as it was called, and the start of the coalface. We saw the monster for the first time. Its arrays of tungsten carbide cutting picks were shiny, sharp and menacing and it seemed to sigh as we approached it, or perhaps that was our imagination.

"Fucking hell" Mitch said, "you wouldn't want that bloody thing chasing you!"

We gingerly got into position between the pan, the conveyer, and the coalface, but there was no one to tell us what to do. Here all the props were Dowty hydraulic, heavy and very well made. All the prop men had gathered ready to start supporting the roof when the cutter set off. It was driven by electricity supplied by an armour-plated steel cable covered over with a thick rubber casing. The cutter operator was in the stable area with his control panel – we never saw him, come to think about it. We had to be just the right distance behind the cutter – if we were too close, huge lumps of coal which fell off it could cause us cuts and serious injury, and if we fell back too far the conveyer pan would crush our legs against the coalface. Unfortunately it travelled too fast for the roof supporters to keep up, so the roof was unsupported for great distances. This was before the automatic advancing roof support systems which were brought in much later. It was all very scary; we could see cracks appear along the roof and fine dust would be dribbling out of them. Was this worth the extra money, I wondered?

After a while we got used to working together and would take it in turns to be in front, next to the cutter. The front man would shift all the big coals with gloved hands and the second man would clean up with the shovel. I gave up my stint and we both worked on the trepanner face full time.

Mitch was quite a guy. His lunch, or 'snap' as it was called, was a whole loaf of white bread, one of those oblong types, not a huge loaf but big enough, and it was wrapped in newspaper along with half a pound of best butter. He would break open the full length of the loaf with his hands and rub the whole half a pound of butter, which was soft from the ambient temperature, down the middle of the bread with his fingers, so you could see three wavy black finger tracks in the butter. Then an onion would suddenly appear like a conjuror's ball. This was smashed on the heel of his boot and the inner part placed in the butter tracks, and that was it, that's what he had every day apart from the day we could have lost our lives. That day he had a massive chunk of cheese in his bread as well. I felt like a pansy with my neatly-packed pork dripping sandwiches. We worked hard and looked after each other, when you rely on each other you become more like family.

Halfway through a shift one day, strange things started to happen. I noticed there was a lot more dust than usual falling from the roof cracks, then the floor started rising up at the edge of the coalface and I could see it flaking and crumbling. It was surprising how soft the floor and the roof were, and I could never quite understand it. This wasn't a cause for concern as it happened quite a lot. The automatic prop trays in the gobblings (this was the area where the coal had been extracted – on this particular coalface it was allowed to collapse once the props were removed) seemed to be getting smaller. Because of the noise and all the dust given off by the cutter we couldn't hear anything and seeing wasn't very good either – the only light was from our headlamps.

Things just didn't seem quite right somehow, and I had a strange feeling but couldn't explain it. Then something caught my eye in the distance, it was one of the prop men. He was a long way from us and he was flashing a light at us, shouting something and beckoning with his lamp to go to him. It was now obvious that something was seriously wrong; we were the only men anywhere near the cutter. The floor had come up and the roof had come down, either one of the two or both, about a foot, and was distorting the chain pan and stopping it from moving over to the coalface. I grabbed Mitch's arm and indicated to him by signs to get out quick, then scrambled over the pan. If it was possible to run on our knees, that's exactly what we did. Looking back, I saw Mitch was struggling and not making any headway. I ran on my knees back to him and saw that his metal toe cap was caught on one of the steel bars (flights) which was travelling along the pan. He couldn't crawl backwards fast enough to unhook it and was being dragged by his metal toecap towards the cutter.

I managed to free him just in time and we were off like shit off a stick. When we were far enough away from the cutter, we could hear men shouting, and the hydraulic props were screaming like some unearthly creature. Hot oil from them was being forced out at immense pressure. I felt a squirt of this oil on my shoulder – it went straight through my shirt and I'm sure it entered my skin as it was so painful for a long time after. If it had entered my eye at that sort of pressure it would have blinded me.

The space we were in was visibly getting smaller. I thought, bloody hell, we could become fossils here. I could actually see the props being forced into the floor and roof at the same time, and the wooden blocks put on top of the props to cushion and stop them from slipping had vanished into the roof.

We reached the huddle of flashing headlights and found that there were eleven men or more all trying to get through the three-foot square hole into the tailgate. They all took their turn in a gentlemanly fashion, but I could feel the immense tension building. There was a lot of hysterical shouting but I could not understand what was being said – men's voices tend to get high pitched when they are afraid.

By now the grey dust was raining down on us from the cracks in the roof as the rock was being ground by tremendous forces into fine dust. Just imagine – there was almost a mile of rock bearing down on us. Waiting our turn to get out was almost unbearable. Thankfully we all got out and were accounted for, and everyone began wondering what would happen next. Then we heard deep thunderous thuds and felt strong gusts of air coming from the hole we had just got out of. Fearing this could affect the tailgate, we left the area fast and headed back to the pit bottom, riding the wide rubber conveyer belts, which ran for miles – they were the life blood of the coal mine as they brought the coal out. The next day we learnt the coalface was a complete write off. Everything was gone, all encased forever in solid rock. I said to Mitch, "You know mate that was a brand-new shovel I've just lost, only bought it last week, crushed."

"Yes, and so could we have been" he said thoughtfully. Then he added "I shouldn't have had that cheese you know".

"Why, that couldn't have caused this?"

"I know that, you daft bugger" he said, "it gave me rampant indigestion."

It turned out that we had hit a massive geological fault line, which had caused the rocks to line up and slide. That was what had caused such catastrophic forces and weight to bear down on the workings, burying everything, coal cutter, the lot. The coalface was a complete loss. This is not the book to go into the technicalities of geology, but nevertheless, it's a very interesting subject.

Back on the market and cleaning up other miners' stints, I was into all sorts of ways of getting my wage back up as near as possible to what it had been. They included earning a few extra pounds carrying the shot firer's explosives in a neat little bag made entirely of conveyer belt material. The detonators and the explosives were not allowed to be carried on one and the same person for obvious reasons. I very rarely saw Mitch and I don't know what happened to him. Cleaning up stints meant I had to work nights and so I was on the night shift all the time. In winter I would go months without seeing the sun. My skin was anaemic lily white, black bags under my eyes, and I was beginning to look like a zombie.

On the bus going home in the early hours there was the usual chorus of the older miners coughing their lungs out while they still smoked their cigarettes. If you had a mate on the opposite shift he would have a lit cigarette waiting for you when you met him in the pithead baths, as they were called. It was hard to imagine that these men were physically fit body-wise from hard manual work, but sadly years of smoking and inhaling dust were taking their toll on their lungs. I remember thinking 'I don't want to get like that if I can help it'.

When miners didn't finish their nine-yard stint it wasn't from idleness, but mainly from illness or unseen problems. For instance, massive lumps of coal could come past you on the conveyer belt – battleships we used to call them. Now if they came halfway off the conveyer and got caught on a couple of props, this caused them to get trapped across the conveyer and nothing would stop the conveyer and tons of coal would spill into your stint in a very short time. Coal would pile up onto the battleship, making it very difficult to get at it with a hammer to break it up, and it could take half a day or more getting it going and cleared up, and all the time more coal was spilling into your stint. What made this problem worse was if someone had shat on the conveyer belt, which was often the case, you got that as well. If your stint wasn't cleared, pay would be deducted. It was best to have a good look at the conveyer belt rollers when you entered your stint. If any of the rollers dipped down towards your stint, it meant the coal would lean over and large coals could fall off and cause the above to happen. Of course, this comes with experience, and chocking up the rollers and making them level was the first thing I did.

However, I now knew that my days down the mine were numbered. Although I enjoyed the high wages, my quality of life was deteriorating, even though I was very fit, and I thought there had to be more to life than this. One day I reported to work as usual and on the token board was a message for me to report to the union office. The token was a brass disc with my number stamped on it. I picked it up from a numbered board in the lamp room, where I also obtained my personal lamp with its lead acid battery all charged up, then gave the token to the man at the pit shaft gate – this was a way of making sure whoever went down was accounted for. I reported to the union office and was greeted by two very large bellied men. Is it just me or why do all union officials seem to be endomorphs? The bigger one said, "I see you 'ent paid any union dues lad."

"Arr well no, I didn't think I had to" I said.

"Well ya bloody well do, so start next week, right?" I did not like his tone, which had a very aggressive manner about it and got my back up. That helped me make up my mind and I left the coalmining industry. I knew that wages like that would be hard to find elsewhere, but I was a qualified miner and could always go back.

Chapter 4

Moving on

~~~~~~

After leaving the mine I went to work with my oldest brother, Fred. He hadn't any transport at that time, but I did, so I stood in to help him out. I now had a Morris Minor Traveller, the one with wooden trim on the bodywork at the back and sides.

Fred was a self-employed contract farmer and we went around farms offering to riddle and bag their stored potatoes which had been buried, as well as any other work that was on offer. Farmers would store their potatoes in a trench dug out in a corner of a field, covered with straw that was put on in a simple thatch pattern and then covered over with about two feet of earth. This would keep them over the winter. If this was done right the potatoes would be nice and dry, free from frost and ready to sell when the farmer could get a better price. It made perfect sense, but some farmers got it very wrong and all that was in the pie was a load of stinking, rotting spuds not even fit for animal food.

It was really hard work, from six in the morning till eight or nine in the evening. In good busy times, we would employ other workers, mostly women, who were good at sorting the potatoes on the riddles before bagging, but we only employed them for the odd day and that wasn't very often. Our pay was £1 per ton and that included riddling, sorting, bagging, weighing and stacking onto a trailer. It was back-breaking work for so little compared to the sort of money I had been earning down the mine but in those days, it was still good money.

In the morning we would stop off at the butcher's on our way to work and buy the biggest beefsteaks available for our lunch break, and we would cook them on an open fire in a large frying pan with a pan of boiled potatoes straight out of the pie – fantastic! But then the Irish labourers moved in and did the work for less, so we lost most of our contracts. Other work we carried out included flax pulling, hedge laying and striking out, which was weeding around sugar beet or other vegetable crops.

One occasion I remember well was when we were working on a farm near Derbyshire and we ran out of petrol getting there with just about two miles to go and a hundred yards from a garage. None of us had any money, but a worker and mate of mine who was with us had a fine-looking watch, so we decided that perhaps we could get some petrol on the strength of the watch. The only container we had was an empty glass milk bottle, but we all walked to the garage and managed to get the bottle filled. The bloke at the petrol station said, "Well I think I've seen just about every bloody thing now."

We got to the farm and found out what we had to do; there was a haystack in a large Dutch barn and we had to take it down and run it through a baling machine. When we were about halfway down, rats were running all over the place, so the farmer called in the local ratcatcher.

When we were three-quarters of the way down the stack, the ratcatcher turned up on an old butcher's bike with his Jack Russell dog in a basket on the front. He put up a fine mesh fence about four feet high all around the stack, and then he and his dog got inside it. It was fascinating to see. The ratcatcher looked like he had just stepped out of a Charles Dickens tale, and with his trousers tied just below the knee and cycle clips around his ankles he was well protected – you wouldn't want a rat running up your leg, would you? He and his dog worked very fast and rats were screaming and bouncing off the net fence, it was like they had suddenly gone stark raving bonkers. The catcher was grabbing the rats two and three at a time. Some hung off the flesh between his thumb and forefinger and then he would bite the neck and pull – it was a wonder this chap didn't go down with some horrible disease or something. He killed the rats by hitting them with a big rusty old spanner, banging their heads on a house brick and biting their necks, so his hands were covered in blood, but it didn't seem to bother him at all.

It was like an old-fashioned theatre, him and his dog being the cast with us, perched on high ground, the audience looking down. The Jack Russell ran around snapping at them and killing with a single bite and a shake. The dog at one moment had one rat in its mouth and two hanging from its jowls. Rats go crazy when they are trapped in a confined space and I'm not surprised with those two maniacs chasing them. There must have been hundreds of rats coming out of that stack, I have never seen the like. Ratcatchers got paid 'a bob a knob' – a shilling, that's five pence, for every tail – and it could be quite profitable in a situation like that.

When he had finished, he gathered all his rats up into sack bags and tied them up. We finished the rest of the stack and agreed we had enough for one day, so we headed home. It was a dirty, smelly old farm, and the stink got into our clothing and stayed with us.

We promised the farmer we would go back in three days' time. Having been paid we got the watch back from the garage. I think the garage man was a bit disappointed having to give the watch back, but it was part of the deal. Then he said, "What's that bloody smell?"

"You don't want to know" Fred said.

We arrived at the farm bright and early after three days' rest and set about striking out (weeding) a two-acre field of cabbage. As the day got hotter, we noticed a different smell from the normal farm pong which got stronger as the day wore on. When it was just about unbearable, we investigated and found it was the rats. The troll, as we called the ratcatcher, had hung up all his rats by piercing their tails on a barbed wire fence so the farmer could count them. The stink was totally unacceptable and as we approached there was a loud drone as thousands of flies suddenly took off. We finished the job as quickly as we could, got paid and left in a hurry. My brother carried on scraping a living at farm work, but for me it was time to move on once more.

Two days later I got my National Service call-up papers. Because I had left the mining industry, I was now eligible for the call up. Oh bugger, I must have been the last one in the country, because they scrapped the call-up on what seemed like the next day.

Off I went to the service call-up centre in Mansfield to find out what I had to do and what was available. I fancied going into the Royal Navy but had to sign on for twenty-two years and that was too long. I could just do the two years' service in the Army but no, if I signed on for six years I'd have more money and would be shipped overseas after my basic training, also I would have money to send home to my mum. I signed on and accepted the Queen's two shillings, which was part of the deal. I chose my local regiment, the First Battalion the Sherwood Foresters, who were stationed in Normanton Barracks, Derbyshire. They were also known as the Notts & Derby regiment and the

Notts and Jocks, because there was a healthy contingent of Scottish guys in the mob.

I attended the army medical centre and had all the usual tests, ears, nose, throat, sight and the hitting of the knee thing. There were about a dozen men in all and the next test involved stripping off completely, which didn't bother me as I was used to it, having been a miner, but most of the guys felt shy and vulnerable holding their hands in front of them and their heads bent low not looking at anybody. We all had to stand in line and the doctor, dressed in a white coat, came along the line lifting in turn each and everyone's penis up with his pencil: "Cough," and then "Bend down and touch your toes". I felt like saying "would you mind washing your pencil before you lift mine," but I didn't.

That was it. A few days later I got a letter saying I had passed the medical and was to report to Normanton Barracks in Derbyshire. I left my lovely Morris Minor Traveller with Fred to help him with his business.

The training was long, hard and strict, and sleeping in a barrack room with forty other men and only eighteen inches between each bed took some getting used to, especially when an NCO burst into the room every day at what seemed like the early hours of the morning shouting "Hands off cocks and onto socks!" at the top of his voice and banging the bottom of each and every metal bedstead with his stick as he walked through the room. I even started to miss coalmining, it was that bad. I'm not going into all the stupid things we had to do in training, but later on I realised it was all to do with discipline and being ready to carry out an order without question, instantly.

My mum and some other members of the family turned up for my passing-out parade. She was very proud and for this occasion she wore her mink coat and fox fur, so it must have been important for her. As for me, I was very pleased to have the training behind me.

After two weeks leave, our Draft DATTT, as we were now called, was heading down to Southampton by train to join the battalion on active service in Malaya. The ship we were to embark on was a 12,598-ton troop carrier, the HMT *Dilwara*, built in Glasgow in 1935. It looked like the whole of the British armed forces were getting on this ship.

My mum and sisters came to Southampton to see me off and I spent an hour or so with them before I had to report for embarkation. Looking down from the ship were the troops' relations, and there were thousands of them, all waving. They looked so very small and I desperately searched the crowd for my mum and sisters. I was beginning to panic and an overwhelming feeling of abandonment was gripping my stomach when I caught sight of them just as the mooring ropes were being hauled aboard. I felt much better after finding them and waving goodbye, but I still had a lump in my throat and wet eyes. I didn't know if I would ever see them again, or they see me for that matter. I carried on waving until they disappeared from view. It would be three years or more before I could hopefully see them again.

Life on board was quite interesting, although we were packed like sardines, it was all part of the adventure, or nightmare, whichever way you look at it. As we got out into the real ocean and out of sight of land, we settled down. We would muster on the deck each morning for general orders, fire drill, lifeboat stations and there was lots to do like clay pigeon shooting and rifle practice with red balloons thrown off the stern of the ship. It was surprising how difficult it was to hit them, but I was a marksman with the badge to prove it. I was playing cards, drinking beer and generally getting on with it.

During a spell of rough weather, which seemed to last for days, there was a lot of seasickness on board and just about everyone was suffering from it. If you went to the side, you risked being hit by other people's vomit blown on the wind. Often I would flick a piece of rolled up tomato skin off my shirt.

I made my way down the metal and tile stairs to the toilet block, a large rectangular room, at both ends of which were the toilets, about five at each end. In the middle of the room was a floor to ceiling wall with sink basins on both sides. All the walls and floor were ceramic tiles and apart from the movement it was hard to imagine you were on a ship. All the sinks were occupied, so I waited at the bottom of the stairwell. I could not believe what I was seeing. The ship was pitching fore and aft, and when it pitched forward all the shavers backed away from the sinks, all the half doors of the toilets swung open and all the shitters came shuffling out, still in their crapping position with their trousers around the ankles. When the ship pitched aft the same thing happened on the other side of the room. I got my turn at a sink and I realised you could not help but go with the motion of the ship. Also moving about was all the vomit and splashed water washing across the floor in little waves, which got up to the first lace hole of my plimsolls. Bits of tomato skin, pea skins, and some unrecognisable food objects made a tidemark around my footwear.

As we sailed into warmer waters life on board felt much more like being in holiday mode, and fitness training on deck was now a regular activity. We had films and lectures about venereal disease (VD) and its effects, which were enough to put anyone off sex for life.

We went ashore at Gibraltar and I got my first experience of a foreign country. It smelt so different. The bars were open all day and night and we saw jaw-droppingly beautiful girls in the bars who were obviously on the game. Narrow streets with rope lines full of washing stretched from one side of the street to an open window on the other side, and women were leaning out of the windows shouting at each other. We didn't have much time, but there was enough to climb the rock and meet the nasty-tempered monkeys who think they own the place. Looking down on the harbour, HMS *Ark Royal* was moored in the bay, and what a fantastic sight she was. It made you so proud to be British.

The next port of call was Cyprus. It was very hot by now and one unfortunate lad got himself so severely sunburnt he had to have hospital treatment, on top of which he was charged with self-inflicted wounds, a serious offence in the Army.

I spent a lot of time looking out to sea watching dolphins keeping pace with the ship and they were hardly moving a fin. One day I saw a manta ray, which was so big that at first I thought it was a sandbank in the middle of the ocean; one wing was up one wave and the other wing up another.

We were now approaching Port Said, which is at the mouth of the Suez Canal. The Suez crisis was evident from the amount of shipping sunk near the entrance, and you could see the masts at an angle poking above the sea. The captain's voice came over the Tannoy system saying we were about to enter a very sensitive area and we should not wave or show any emotion in any way whatsoever. The ship filled the canal with very little room to spare, and on reflection it must have been a nightmare navigating a ship that size down such a narrow channel. The sea was the same colour as the desert sand and it must have looked quite strange, a massive ship crossing a desert dwarfing everything in sight.

The banks were lined with angry people shouting and waving their fists at us, but I was more interested in the huge black fin following in the wake of the ship. It stood out in contrast to the sand-coloured water. I often stood at the stern of the ship watching the wake disappear over the horizon. If it was a shark then it was a big one. Of course I had never seen a shark before, but it must have been getting some kind of living from the ship's jettisoned galley waste, the odd chicken leg or whatever, and it crossed my mind that perhaps it was waiting for someone to fall overboard.

The ship continued its journey into the Red Sea and on to Aden. We moored offshore and were soon surrounded by bumboats, with these guys who sell everything and anything. They throw a line up to you with a bag attached and you haul up what you want to see and inspect, then you send the money down to them in the bag if you buy it. I bought a brand-new solid gold Rolex watch for two pounds! By the time I got to Singapore it was rusty red inside and out, another lesson learnt.

Then it was from the Gulf of Aden to the Arabian Sea and on to Colombo, the capital of Ceylon as it was known then and is of course now Sri Lanka. There were constant lightning storms at night from all directions, but I could not hear any thunder; it was mostly sheet lightning, probably a long way off. We were allowed ashore at Colombo for a short time and I visited the Mount Lavinia Hotel with its wonderful British colonial heritage – this is where one of the Bond films was made later. Oh, and yes, a mate and I fell for the next trick hook line and sinker. A taxi driver said he would take us to see a woman go with a donkey! We had heard about it on board ship, so off we went. He took us to the top of a hill about three miles away and said, "You pay me now, John." We could see the ship and everyone making their way back on board. "You pay me now John, I take you back to ship." What a con, and we fell for it. This guy was a true professional and knew exactly how long the ship stayed in port. We had no time to argue so we paid. Yet another lesson learnt.

When we finally docked in Singapore we had been at sea for just over a month and the air was full of sweet-smelling spices drifting out to us from the land. The port was very busy and from our height the people looked like ants running about, with small thin men carrying hessian covered loads as big as themselves on their heads. Two wheeled handcarts weaving in and out of the traffic carried everything from bananas to cane cages crammed full of live chickens.

Our draft was transported to a transit camp in preparation for joining the battalion. Here we were acclimatised and got to know most of the local biting bugs that fly and crawl. We had more lectures about the enemy, the jungle, and areas that were strictly out of bounds in Singapore such as Shanty Town, Boogie Street and Black Alley. Of course, these where the first places we went to once we were let loose, as prostitutes were ten a penny.

I spent a lot of my time in the famous Brianna Club. It was a great attraction for all the armed forces in Singapore and you could go there and totally chill out; it was like a bit of old Blighty right in the middle of town. The city in those days was quite a smelly old place with open sewers running through the town, which had once been rivers. Beautiful girls would spit in the streets just like ill-mannered navvies. Prostitutes thronged the covered walkways and it seemed like all the girls in town were on the game. I have since learnt it's a beautiful, clean, thriving and well-organised place to visit now and totally different from when I was there, and spitting is prohibited.

Quinine was issued each morning as an antimalarial drug along with salt tablets, which were taken in front of the issuing NCO just to make sure you took them.

We were now kitted up with our full jungle gear including an eighteen-inch golluk, which was a machete or jungle knife, and water purifying tablets which turned pea-green water into grey water. All rank insignia were removed from clothing as a precaution against capture. A green floppy hat with a bright yellow cross sewn on the front and back was issued, for identification in a jungle environment only.

Eventually, after intense training, we moved up into Malaya, a place called Johor Bahru, where we joined the battalion and did some more serious jungle training.

Being an ex-miner, I seemed to be fitter than most and could take whatever physical training tests they could throw at me. I could climb a rope using just one arm and my legs. I would run at least two miles in the morning before breakfast and three or four miles in the evening every day.

On one occasion as I was running through a rubber plantation, I ran over a hill and down into a valley and accidently ran into a family of wild hogs. They panicked and scattered in all directions screaming and making one hell of a noise, but nobody was more surprised than me. Then the big male hog realised it was only a human thing, and came running back towards me with its tail standing erect, grunting and flashing its fangs. I knew he could outrun me with ease, so the only place to go was up a rubber tree. In my haste I knocked off the little cup from which the rubber tappers collect the latex. The first branch was about ten feet up, and here I was able to wait and have a good look at him. This animal was all muscle, a powerful head with tusks like fangs sticking up from its lower jaw, and he would have made mincemeat of me. He tried to look up at me, but his neck wasn't designed for looking up, it was too thick and muscular; all he could do was turn his head slightly and give me a nasty one-eyed look.

He hung around grunting and prancing round the tree then after what seemed like hours, but was probably no more than a couple of minutes, he realised his family wasn't coming back so he gave up and ran off to find them. I was absolutely lathered in rubber latex.

Quite often when running through rubber plantations I would run into a giant spider's web, which could span from one tree to the next. They are the golden orb weaver spider, as big as a man's hand with its legs. One once spanned my entire face as it was in the centre of its web when I ran into it. They are quite harmless but they do have huge fangs and I wouldn't trust them at all, especially knowing the females eat the males after mating.

All the buildings had their share of geckos, which are little lizards and look just like our freshwater newts. They would run up the walls and over the ceiling, preying on insects attracted by lights. In the city, restaurants, posh hotels and even government buildings all had geckos running over the ceilings. They could walk on any surface from glass to canvas and they would crap on the people below – not a lot but enough. Sometimes without any warning they would go absolutely bonkers, fall off the ceiling, jump about, roll over, shed their tail and drop dead, but the tail carried on wriggling, all for no apparent reason other than to distract a would-be predator. It could be somewhat disconcerting if you happened to be in bed when they dropped on you.

A Special Forces unit of the SAS (Special Air Service), greatly reduced in numbers after the war, had been re-formed in 1952 and called the Malay Scouts Squadron. Later it was re-named 22 SAS and we were trained by them in jungle warfare. This unit sounded exciting and adventurous, although we knew very little about it. What we did know was that you had to be extremely fit to be even considered, so a mate and I approached the Commanding Officer through the usual channels and applied for a transfer. He said he would consider our application and let us know in due course, but he also reminded us we were on active service and it was not a good time to be leaving the battalion.

A couple of days later we were summoned to attend Commanding Officer's orders. We were in our best uniform and were marched in. "I've considered your request for a transfer and I have turned it down," he said. "However, I am sending you both on a physical training course run by the Physical Training Corps." This was at the Far East

Land Forces Headquarters in Singapore, and that was it. We were to train as PT Instructors with a minimum starting rank of lance corporal, becoming full-blown corporals on completion of the course.

It was a gruelling eight weeks of solid physical and mental ability training, including the study of anatomy and physiology. The course contained the best and fittest from several forces, the Malay Regiment, RAF, Navy, Australian Army and more. We were on the go morning to evening non-stop with lots of work over the assault course and other torture equipment.

Towards the end of the course I realised I had a big problem; I couldn't swim on the surface. Yes, I could swim but only under water – swimming on the surface or treading water I could not do, and this was a requirement on the course. For the swimming test you had to be fully clothed and carrying a backpack with two house bricks inside, boots tied by the laces and hung around the neck and a dummy rifle of an equivalent weight to be carried without getting it too wet. The test was to swim a length of the full-size pool, tread water for two minutes and then climb out. I was horrified, and I confessed my problem to a mate. "I might as well pack my bags now" I said, "There is no way I can do that. I bloody sink, my bones are too heavy."

I could swim the full length of a swimming pool under water, but as soon as I got to the surface I sank. I was a champion high board diver and had spent so much time in the water anyone would have thought I was a great swimmer. I had even spent so much time diving and playing around in the local swimming pool that I had caught a disease of the inner ear called otitis externa, which put me in hospital for well over a month. The common name for this condition was Singapore Ear, a very nasty fungal infection where green pus seeps from the ear and it stinks.

I don't want to go into all the boring aspects of my treatment, but a couple of experiences stuck in my mind. Part of the treatment was carried out by a doctor who wore a round mirror strapped to his forehead. He approached me with a skewer-type metal rod and a long thin bandage soaked in castor oil or something, and expertly filled my entire ear to almost busting point with the wick, as he called it, I had this in both ears every day I was in the British Military Hospital Singapore. The memorable part of all this was the removal of the wick. When I looked at the doctor, all I saw was my own worried face looking back at me in his mirror. He took hold of the wick and with a steady constant pull, removed about a yard of it; the feeling was truly orgasmic, and never have I had a feeling like it. If there are any feeling freaks out there, this is the one for you.

Another memorable aspect, of course, was the pain. They say you don't remember pain – not true, it was so bad I became completely dependent on codeine to relieve it. The tablets were large, the size of a one-pound coin, and they must have contained a lot of morphine because I was well and truly hooked on them. The fantastic nurses gradually reduced my intake and saved me.

To get back to my swimming problem, my mate gave me a lot of encouragement and said we should get training straight away. I had one great asset, I was not afraid of water and always opened my eyes underwater. After about a week's practice whenever we could, usually in the evenings, I was getting the hang of it. An Australian guy got in on the act, Snowy his name was because he had white hair. I told him what the problem was and he burst out with "Struth, mate, I was just the bloody same last year, I was a sinker just like you", and I got the full lowdown on how he had got around it. He was a great help and we all became good mates.

When the time came for the swimming test, a week before the end of the course, I passed, but only just. I was happy to have it behind me so I could concentrate on other things.

Sharing the same headquarters was a contingent of the Women's Royal Army Corps. We were working in the grounds and one of the lessons was taking a tree on physical training. Each man in turn stood in front of the tree and shouted commands and demonstrated the exercises, and we even had to correct the tree as if it had got it wrong. Of course, when it was my turn all the WRACs were walking past laughing and shouting, which reminded me of my factory days. We both passed with flying colours and re-joined the battalion as full-blown corporals, but some poor guys never made the grade and so failed the course.

Arriving back at base, my boss was a staff sergeant of the Physical Training Corps and I was made second in command. My first job was to build two huge A frames with a cross member and ropes attached for climbing, to form part of an assault course using trees cut from the jungle. It was quite a project, and I got a mention from the commanding officer for my efforts.

My classes were up to eighty men all spread out in formation, and with such a large class I got my colleague to help. I would start off with basic groundwork such as press-ups. The guys at the very back thought they could get away without doing anything, but I was on to them and put the skivers where I could see them. Being in front of such a vast number of soldiers and expecting them to do what I commanded was quite daunting to say the least, at first that is, and there was always one who tried to disrupt the guys around him. I would stop the exercise, bring him out to the front of the class and tell him to take over. There was total silence, and it worked every time.

One day the base camp at Johor Bahru was hit by a tornado, also known as a land hurricane. It was very sudden and no one was prepared. I was on the sports field, a busy time for me, getting ready for the annual PTET tests. This was a time when the whole battalion was tested on its physical fitness, and that meant everyone including officers. A detailed report of each man's physical capabilities was sent to the commanding officer, and if anyone was below standard, they were sent to me for a couple of week's solid training.

The first thing to happen were hailstones the size of golf balls bouncing off the grass, and everyone ran for cover. When the wind came it was deafening. Enormous trees were snapped off like matchsticks, and leaves and twigs were blasted at me as if from a shotgun and corrugated tin roof sheets flew around - they could have taken your head off. The only safe place to shelter for me out in the open was the two-foot deep monsoon drains, and that's where I lay on my stomach, but I had to get to my little hut as the hailstones were very painful. It only lasted for a few minutes, but the devastation was immense with hardly a basha left standing. The chawalla's (tea maker) tin shed had gone and so had his tick book with all the names of men owing him for tea and egg butties (fried egg sandwiches). He was crying openly, but the poor sod got no sympathy. Just about everyone was affected in some way or other. The camp eventually returned to normal and the tests resumed the next day.

First job each morning was getting rid of all the scorpions from under the training mats. They were the big black ones, which were not as dangerous as the small sandy-colored ones, but they could still give you a big arm if they stung you. Route marches in full battle dress including arms and ammunition were the most dreaded test of all and many failed, especially the GHQ (headquarters) personnel. I felt sorry for them as their job was in an office all day and as a result their fitness suffered. I must say some of them made a great effort in the evening playing games.

We were training on the sports field for the big games where many regiments competed against each other, and my job was to advise and teach technique to various groups such as discus, shot put and javelin. I was passing the long jump contenders when the officer in charge of that little group asked me if I had done any long jumping. "Only when my boss kicks my ass," I said jokingly "But I'll give it a go." I ran down the track and my jump was over four foot longer than their best man. I was surprised myself, but tried not to show it. The officer begged me to join his team, so I did, and represented the battalion at the games. I did very well out of three jumps and my best was only inches from the Olympic record. The other two jumps were disqualified. I later heard that a black guy in America had just put about six foot on the world record, so that was my hopes dashed.

I was standing around just looking at the discus throwing when I heard a loud pop followed by a scream. I turned around and saw a guy limping along with a javelin through his lower leg, protruding about eight inches through near the gastrocnemius (calf muscle). I ran up to him. He was a big guy of African origin whose name was Xavier and he was gripping the javelin with both hands hopping about. The strange thing was he didn't pull the javelin out, he pulled his leg off the javelin. The chap who had thrown the javelin was very upset, but he still got a big bollocking for not sticking to the designated throwing area. The wounded guy was very lucky that the javelin had gone through the layer of fat between the muscles, so no real harm was done.

I did a lot of cross county running in those days against the RAF and the Gurkha regiment and won quite a few cross-country six-mile races, though they didn't include the Gurkhas – nobody could beat them at cross county and the hillier the better for them, but when it was a three-mile flat track race they were beaten every time. They come from Nepal, a very mountainous region in India, so they were quite used to running up hills. They were short, stocky guys so running up hills, was like they were in a low gear.

At a certain time of year, the termites swarmed and poured from their nests by the millions – like ants, they acquired wings for breeding purposes. As this phenomenon usually happened at night, they would head straight for any source of light, usually hanging kerosene lamps. The only way to get rid of them was to place a bowl of water under each lamp. They would be attracted to the light reflection in the water, fly in and drown. In a short period of time there were millions and the water was thick with them. I think they would have made a very good soup, but I've never been that hungry.

Chapter 5

In the jungle

~~~~~

My first experience of the real jungle was quite an eye opener. Oh, I had done all the training, gone to all the survival lectures, but it all seemed to be part of some protective shield and nothing could happen to us, after all we were British. When the time came to do the job we had all been training for, it had a very concentrating effect on the mind. Suddenly we were there, this was the real thing, and any of us could be shot at any moment, though the thought that someone out there would be trying to kill us didn't seem right. But of course, it was very real and when we heard about casualties in other units it got even more real.

What I noticed most of all was heightened senses, sensitive

smell and hearing and a strong awareness of surroundings – I wish I had them now! We were fighting an enemy who was so used to the jungle they could just disappear; they were immune to the local diseases, which was just as well as they didn't have medical equipment, but they could live off what the jungle had to offer. If their numbers had been significantly greater, then we would have had a real problem on our hands. They rarely left the security of the jungle, but they did attack the one and only train that ran the length of the country, along with small kampongs and small local police stations as well as estate owners, and rubber plantations.

Bloodsuckers, and I don't mean the government or the taxman. I'm talking about leeches of the Malayan jungle, lean wiry creatures, about two inches long. Nothing like the leeches on Humphrey Bogart's back in the film *African Queen*, they were more like medical leeches. Malayan leeches don't even need water. They hang off bushes and wait under the leaf litter on the jungle floor, which is always damp and very spongy. When an animal or a man sat on the ground, the leeches emerged from under the rotting leaf litter and homed in on the heartbeat or, with a lot of bloodsuckers, they could detect the carbon dioxide in the exhaled breath. The heartbeat was transmitted down the body and through the soggy ground – well that's my theory. They looped their way straight for our bootlace holes. They also got onto us from trees, so they did have lots of opportunities. How they got inside our pants I had no idea, but I went to great lengths to keep them out. When I saw them probing my bootlace holes, I would quickly flick them away. Burning them with a cigarette didn't work, especially in the jungle where smoking wasn't even allowed, and I found insect repellent or lighter fuel dabbed on the mouthparts worked the best. However, they did get inside and when they did, for some reason known only to them, they always went for the warmest part of the body, between our legs. We wouldn't feel a thing! The bite was shaped like the letter 'Y' and they would hang there and suck blood until they were almost spherical before dropping off.

Normally, if leeches were preying on animals, they would just drop to the ground and be ready to breed, having had a meal of blood. Now the only way we realised that leeches had been feeding on us was when there was a warm sticky feeling between our toes. It was our own blood! The leeches had dropped down our trouser leg as fat round balls and been squashed by our feet. They don't have a skeleton, the only bones they have are three teeth that form a triangle, hence the strange bite pattern.

The more serious aspect of leech bites was the loss of blood. When a leech bites, it injects an anticoagulant into the bloodstream. This keeps the wound bleeding for hours even after the leech has dropped off. Then there is the problem of the bites becoming infected and turning into ulcers. In such humid conditions the skin never dries and it becomes very soft, white and prune-like. With your skin in this condition it seems every creature is out to bite and suck on you.

After three or four weeks in the jungle, which was about all the body could take, we got the chance to recuperate at the main base camp for about ten days, where we could get rid of all our ticks, lice and sores and harden the skin in the sun. The next task was getting our weapons cleaned, freed of rust and ready for action. In such conditions our firearms demanded constant attention. A wonderful weapon to have in the jungle was the repeating shotgun which had one up the barrel and six in the stock. Using heavy shot, it could blast a hole a yard wide though the undergrowth, so aiming the gun accurately was not a problem. We only got to use one of these when we were either a leading shotgun or tail end Charlie, the last man of the petrol.

We were shipped up country, as the communist guerrilla terrorist organisation was reported to be on the move and it was feared that they had come from the border area, and that could mean a fresh infiltration of the enemy forces. We arrived at the arranged position and were met by an artillery major. They had setup their heavy artillery guns facing the direction in which we were to enter the jungle. The major told us they would fire over our heads into the jungle and hope the enemy would run into us. I didn't like the idea at all and told him this enemy was not daft, but he outranked us so that was it, in we went.

We were on rocky ground and had to go down a valley through very rugged terrain to get up to the jungle. The shells flew overhead with a terrifying noise like screams from hell. The artillery stopped firing when we reached the jungle's edge – thank God for that, I thought. As we made our way through the jungle we came upon the area where the shells had struck, and it was devastating. The trees had been shattered into a million splinters - it was total destruction and impossible to get through it. I could not understand what could be achieved by such action as the area was completely impenetrable. We were supposed to move south, but it was impossible without first getting out of the jungle and skirting around the shelled area. Here we re-entered the jungle and continued to search for the enemy, but progress was painfully slow, and if we were able to cover half a mile in a day that was extremely good going.

The tracker, who was a Sarawak ranger from Borneo, picked up a fresh trail. He pointed to the ground and we bent low to see what he was looking at. He said with his fingers and gestures which looked quite rude, "Two men, one hour." We looked very hard and even tried to imagine what he could see. I thought I was a good tracker, but this one beat me. We set off with renewed vigour and anticipation, everyone paying full attention to his surroundings.

The tracker stopped again, examining the ground very carefully and feeling the plants with the back of his hand. "Pig one hour" he said, and pointed in the direction it had gone. We moved on a little further and the Sarawak tracker became very interested in a bent leaf. He waved us down and we all took up defensive positions on one knee and stayed like this for twenty minutes or more, just listening. Our circulation was impaired by having to stay in this position for any length of time and standing was quite painful.

Then there was movement in the undergrowth and weapons were very slowly brought to the firing position. It was not possible to make out where the movement noise was coming from, it seemed to be all around us. Suddenly breaking through the vegetation came two orangutans holding hands. The smaller one was carrying an ugli fruit, a sort of knobby grapefruit, in its mouth. They looked like they had been on a shopping spree and never knew we were there. After they had gone, we all had a good laugh, a nervous laugh with the relief of high tension. We continued our search and found evidence of where the enemy had stayed the night, but that was about all we did find on this particular patrol.

There's a plant in the Malayan jungle called 'wait a minute' – well, that's what we called it. Weaving its way through the undergrowth, it's a beautiful shiny dark green fan-like fern. At its base the centre stem continues to grow away from the main plant and it's almost invisible to see amongst the tangle of vegetation. It has a very long trailing stem, quite thin and covered in vicious backward facing half-inch hooks. It may just as well be made of stainless steel it's so strong. It makes our brambles feel like silk thread in comparison. If it caught your clothing you had to 'wait a minute' and carefully unhook the thing. It took two hands to do this, and if you tried to force your way past, it would simply rip its way through the clothing to your flesh. If the plant had ripped your flesh, in the humidity infection always followed, then the inevitable ulcers that never healed in the jungle climate, and when they did heal you would carry the scar for the rest of your life. Should you have made the mistake of trying to slash it with your prang, jungle machete or gollack, it would almost certainly bounce and spring around, slashing your hands and face. It demanded to be treated with the utmost respect.

I have seen a whole patrol consisting of a Sarawak tracker followed by the leading automatic shotgun bearer (there's no time to take aim in the jungle), the section commander, four men and the tail end Charlie, usually a Gurkha, all stopped in their tracks by strands of 'wait a minute'. They looked like they were performing slow motion ballet while they twisted, bent, turned and stretched with arms held high forming an arch, some with arms low as they passed this seemingly invisible menace, their weapons clasped between their knees. What a perfect opportunity for an enemy terrorist attack!

When night fell in the jungle around about 1900 hours, preparations for the coming darkness had to be completed within twenty minutes, as that's how long it took for it to get pitch black. At the end of a day's patrol, a base camp had to be constructed and a perimeter fence made of vines gathered from the surrounding area had to be attached to the trees at waist height, forming a circle around the camp. These acted as a safety barrier if there was to be any movement at night, and also a guide to the latrines. Fixing the vines in a suitable area we had cleared was brought to a standstill by an enormous monitor lizard which came running and bouncing into the centre of the clearing. It was at least six or seven feet long, and it stood tall and looked around. Some of the men had removed their wet pants and were wearing just a green towel around their waists. The lizard took off in the direction of a towel clad man – I don't think it meant any harm, it just wanted out. Being suddenly surrounded by men, these lizards can really move fast, with its thrashing tail, high-stepping spiky legs and a poisonous bite, so you don't want to stand in its way. The guy panicked and ran into the undergrowth, where his towel was whipped away by a 'wait a minute' plant. The whole patrol was watching as two pumping lily-white backside cheeks disappeared into the jungle. Even the lizard paused momentarily at the spectacle then shot off in a different direction.

Torches were allowed only in a real emergency, and only the section commander had one. It is hard to imagine how dark it got. The only experience I have had of this kind of darkness was in the coalmine where I worked in the 1950s. To sleep in the jungle you must be well off the ground, as snakes, beetles and scorpions sought out sources of heat and it was best to avoid their attention. A creature you had to look out for was the ten-inch-long bright red centipede which came sniffing around at night and liked to get into smelly boots. You didn't want one of those things grazing on your mature cheddar when you put your boots on, as they are very poisonous. You could actually hear them when they ran, a kind of clicking sound, quite unnerving at night.

Two stout poles were cut, trimmed and threaded through pocket seams sewn into a seven-feet by two-feet canvas sheet forming a hammock which was then fixed to convenient trees about two or three feet above the ground. Once, in haste to get my hammock up before dark, I cut a sapling without checking its upper branches, and brought down, right over my head, a red ants' nest. The Malay name for this extremely aggressive ant is 'kerengga' and their nest is a huge ball made of glued-together living leaves. The ants use their own larvae to stick together leaves that are held in place by other ants until the glue hardens, which requires amazing teamwork; they are about three quarters of an inch long. The strange thing about these ants is the queen, who is bright green, a most unusual colour among ants. The males are black and only the workers are red, with black eyes. They have one unique specialist predator, which is the caterpillar of a moth. The moth lays an egg or two underneath the nest on the outside of the ball of leaves. The caterpillar that emerges is flat and oval shaped. It hangs around the outside of the nest until its shell has hardened, then makes its way into the ants' nest. The ants try to bite it and lift it but it's too hard, too flat and low for lifting, and in their attempts they inadvertently coat it with their own pheromones and so the caterpillar is soon free to make its way to the centre of the brood chamber where it feeds by cloaking the ant larvae with its body and eating them alive. I suppose if you're going to eat someone else's babies, its best to do it with discretion.

Of course, it has to go through its metamorphosis stage and become a moth, and when it does so it has a trick or two up its sleeve to get out of the nest. The moth now looks just like any tasty old insect and is immediately attacked, but it is covered with sticky, loose, feathery scales and it can run fast. When the ants attack all they get is a bunch of sticky fibers that gum up their mouth parts, so it leaves a trail of face-cleaning, swearing, bad-tempered ants. When it gets to the nest entrance, it flies away and the cycle starts all over again.

The ants' bite is enriched with formic acid and they bite with large pincers and hang on, so you have to pull off their heads before they let go with their jaws. My first reaction was to protect my eyes, but I'm sure they were biting though my eyelids. A mate quickly cleared my face by rubbing them off with a sweat rag socked in insect repellent, but I was bitten on my nose, in my nose, ears and inside my lips. Yes, they bite like hell and what made it even worse was that I got insect repellent in my eyes and couldn't see a bloody thing for quite some time. Within minutes everyone was slapping their arms and legs, and there was only one thing to do. With thousands of really pissed-off ants, their eggs and larvae on the jungle floor and dark rapidly approaching, we had to move camp quickly and start all over again. I was not very popular that day.

I think I have my dad's ability to spot things most people would walk past, and on this occasion it was a snake. We had just set up camp when I said to a couple of mates "There's a snake in that bush, so be careful." They looked closely and said "that's not a bloody snake, it's a vine."

"I'm telling you it's a snake," I said. I must admit it did look just like a vine but I knew it was a viper and very deadly. They wouldn't have it and argued that it was a vine. "All right I'll prove it, but I warn you it can move very fast, so watch it". The bush was smothered in vines, so the snake was well camouflaged. I poked it with my jungle knife and it burst into life, uncoiling itself at great speed and the guys were jumping about. "Fucking hell man, kill it!" one of the guys shouted. Another guy chopped its head off with a single swipe, and he was about to pick the head up when I said "Don't touch it" and grabbed his arm. I put my knife near its open mouth and its teeth clamped onto the blade, making a squeaking noise on the steel.

If we were lucky enough to get hold of a piece of parachute silk from an aerial food supply drop, then we could fashion a shelter over our hammocks and avoid the constant drip of water, caterpillars and insects from the forest canopy. That was probably the only real creature comfort to be had in the jungle. No wonder guys would go for the parachute silk before touching the food supply, even though it could contain bars of chocolate!

An amazing phenomenon occurred at night on the jungle floor, which at first had a very unsettling effect on our senses. When lying in our hammocks we obviously couldn't see the stars through the canopy of trees as it was over eighty feet high and dense, but the jungle floor slowly became just as the Milky Way is to the sky. It was a mass of cold glowing specks of light very similar to the phosphorescence seen at sea, only this was constantly glowing. If you looked at it for a while, dark shapes moved across, blocking out some of the lights, and you realised something was moving about – the more specks of light were covered, the bigger the creature. If you felt something crawling on you there was a tremendous urge to panic and brush it off as quickly as you could, but this instinct had to be controlled. If it was daylight, you would look to see what it was and bat it off the same way it was crawling. Many insects, and especially the giant centipede, which could be up to ten inches long, had very poisonous spiky legs and to brush them the wrong way was to risk being stabbed by their sharp leg spikes. If you were stabbed, you would be wearing an arm or leg twice the size of your other limbs. At night, it was best to let whatever was crawling on you pass over undisturbed – very difficult to do, believe me. It was sometimes hard to get to sleep and it was best not to know what was moving about, if you wanted to sleep at all.

An essential element of successfully living in the jungle was to try and enjoy it, to be at one with it, to be interested in its diversity of flora and fauna and most of all not to fight it. Living in the jungle was a challenge at the best of times and not all people could cope with it. Because I loved all aspects of animal and insect life right from childhood, I found the whole experience fascinating. Studying insects, collecting specimens and preserving them with an injection of formaldehyde formalin was a great interest of mine.

Although jungle life had its hardships, there were times after spending days in the dank twilight zone with our clothes constantly wet, perspiration unable to evaporate, when we were rewarded by suddenly happening upon a clearing, usually by the side of a fast-flowing river, where the sun got though and dried our clothes and skin. Pools left by the retreating water during the dry season exposed carved bathtub-shaped holes in the rock, making it possible to bathe, wash and dry clothing. But these were also extremely dangerous places as there was little cover and the noise of flowing water masked possible sounds made by the enemy, so constant alertness had to be maintained at all times. Discreet sentries were posted in turn, away from the noise of the river and covering all approaches.

On our way back to the base camp, after studying the map, we decided to take a short cut and follow a small stream. Jungle maps were very ambiguous – not surprising considering we were in virgin jungle and the maps were made up from old aerial photos taken years before, so we could not take them very seriously.

The stream wound its way downward and disappeared into a swamp – well, that was it then. As night was approaching, we decided to retrace our tracks uphill and make camp. In the mud and covering our tracks were huge round footprints – something big had been following us. With weapons at the ready and sentries posted, we made camp. Just before rum ration with the light fading fast, there was this enormous crashing and the soggy ground shook beneath our feet, but it was too dark to investigate. Low grumbling noises were heard throughout the night and I don't think anyone slept much at all.

Next day a mate and I went out with weapons cocked to find what was out there. The ground slid away and levelled out, and there were more footprints, but this time they were big cat-type prints. It looked like something else had been eyeing us up.

Just ahead the jungle gave way to a clearing filled with wild banana plants, the fruits of which were very small, sweet and tasty. We pushed our way through the plants, filling our pockets, but it's difficult to get past these plants without making a noise. Suddenly, the ground trembled and banana plants came crashing down around us. There was a deep grumbling noise and that was enough for us to get the hell out. As we ran uphill towards the camp, a wait-a-minute-plant ripped my pocket away, complete with bananas. A family of jungle elephants – they are much smaller than African elephants and their tusks point inward to allow them to pass through the vegetation – had also found the bananas, so we left them to it.

Back at the camp and after studying the map, we realised

we were near the jungle edge. Well, it was the edge of the tree canopy and in front of us were ten-foot-high belukha, similar to our bracken but much denser and thicker. It was very difficult to get through it as years and years of dead one and a half inch-thick stems had piled up and covered the ground and new stalks had grown through this to form tall, lush, green new ferns. It was like trying to walk through wire wool.

We finally came out onto a rocky outcrop and could see the sky and feel the sun's heat, which was fantastic. But did we itch! Oh my god, every man was covered with ticks. They were only small, but their heads were well buried in our flesh and we could not shift them. We estimated that each man must have had at least two hundred ticks on his body. This was not good. The need to get to base camp was now urgent, as if infection set in we would be in serious trouble.

Out of the jungle, progress was much faster and the sun helped the situation by drying our clothing, but it didn't remove any ticks. We arrived at base camp just in time, as redness was appearing on our flesh around the ticks' heads, which is a sure sign of pending infection. A crude shower system was set up with four shower heads, which were just pipes. Four men would strip off and face the back of the man in front and we did what I have since learnt was the worst thing to do – we cracked the body of each of the ticks with our two thumbs and left the head still in, which simply forced the ticks' body contents into our own bloodstreams.

After the tick cracking session, we washed our bodies with carbolic soap. It was the best part of a week before the ticks' heads started falling off, and we were lucky that no infection and no disease was reported.

At a base camp near the village of Yong Peng in Malacca, three of us decided to go for a swim in a large river that ran through the village. It had broad, gently sloping muddy banks on both sides so it must have been tidal, and the water was mud-coloured and had a strong smell about it. Just past the village it wound itself into impenetrable mangrove swamp and disappeared. After the swim, we climbed out by way of a rickety old pier made of bamboo.

There was an air of sadness throughout the village. A Malay Indian told us that only two days before, a crocodile had taken a small boy. Whenever children or dogs went missing crocodiles were blamed, and for good reason. Had we known this beforehand, swimming would have been off the agenda. Swimming in dirty water was asking for trouble, and we all paid the price. All three of us went down with galloping dysentery and within a short time demand on the one and only bog was overwhelming. It was of a corrugated tin and wooden framed construction with an atap roof (thatched palm) positioned right at the edge of the jungle but near enough to keep the rest of the camp awake for the best part of that night. I'm pretty sure each of us could have shat through the eye of a needle at a hundred yards without touching the sides. Yes, it was that bad.

Each time we visited the bog through the night it was necessary to kick hell out of the tin side and scare all the wildlife out before entering. Bats favored this place to hang whilst consuming their prey and would swoop down, scaring the shit out of you, as if we needed it. Especially when most of what we were desperately trying to get rid of had already gone, but the compulsion to go was just as strong.

The most amazing aspect of all this was the timing. We all got up at exactly the same time from different parts of the camp, and it was a mad rush to the bog – rank was ignored.

During a patrol in the northern sector we came across what we thought were boxes of ammo, partly buried. It turned out to be money dropped by the Japanese just before and during their occupation of Malaya, tightly packed in three-inch bundles protected in green greaseproof wrappings and sealed with wax. It was a beautiful-looking currency, the size of our old twenty-pound notes (of the 1950s) and adorned with the most exotic fruits and flowers imaginable. It was intended to destabilize the local economy during their occupation. I never understood how it could work, but for the moment it was nice to think we were rich, even though the money was worthless. I really wish I had kept some.

On one occasion we came across an enormous python. These non-poisonous snakes are constrictors and can grow up to thirty feet in length. This one was at least twenty-five, but it was just about dead and judging by the swelling in its belly it had swallowed quite a large animal. The Sarawak trackers, of which we had two on this patrol, killed and butchered it with the speed and skill of a surgeon. Its meal had been a wild pig and as our food supplies were very low, enough of the snake was taken to feed the whole patrol. When camp was made, we settled down to a feast of python, a mud turtle from the creek and hardtack biscuits.

Mud turtles are very dangerous creatures to handle. They live in muddy freshwater creeks and feed on frogs, fish and snakes. The neck is long and the head can be shot out with lightning speed, delivering a vicious bite with the creature's pincer-like jaws, so it's like being attacked with a toenail clipper. I found this one in a muddy pool under overhanging roots and it could have cost me a finger or two, so it's just as well I didn't try to catch it myself. Luckily for me a Sarawak tracker also saw it, and he handled it by grasping the edges of the shell just in front of the hind legs, as they can reach anywhere forward of this with their long neck. The turtle was good and tasted a bit like pork, but python is an acquired taste. It was like chicken-flavoured cotton wool with a dash of ammonia, and I think it would have been better to have eaten the pig, even though it had already been eaten.

A two-inch square hardtack biscuit makes a whole slice of bread when soaked in a mess tin of water for about a couple of hours. When we got kitted out with the food rations at base camp, each man was issued with a large box which contained all that was needed to live on for a given length of time in the jungle, and hardtack biscuits made up the bulk. We had self-heating cans of soup and just pulled a tab on the tin and it heated up the contents, and that was in those days! We also had odour-free fuel tablets for our small collapsible stove, jam, porridge, water purifying tablets which made it possible to drink water that was pea green in colour, give it a smell of chlorine and turn it gray, a few more items, and a bar of dark chocolate – this was favoured by everyone and was often eaten before we even got into the jungle. A big mistake a lot of guys made was rejecting the hardtack biscuits and throwing them away, but I took all mine and some to spare. Those same guys after a few days were begging for them back, and the worst part is they never seemed to learn.

Rum, yes, we did get rum rations in the jungle. When I think back, we were not allowed to smoke or wear anything that had a strong smell such as aftershave, soap or things like that because smells hang around and travel at nose height in and throughout the jungle, yet the man carrying the rum ration you could smell for miles. A tot of rum was handed out each night just before dark. Pictures of nude women, compliments on his good looks. Nothing could get that all-important reaction and an extra tot.

There are many kinds of mosquitoes in Malaya, and they all bite. Not all carry malaria, but some carry dengue fever and some yellow fever. The spotted mosquito is the worst carrier of malaria, but the trouble is, they are not always spotted. One sure way of identification is its attitude when at rest. Its body is held obliquely to the surface it's standing on and its bite is slantwise, while all the others stand parallel to the surface of your skin. Not a lot of people know that.

Many of the trees that made up the forest canopy were the giant redwoods – well that's what I called them because of their beautiful dark red sap, but they were probably mahogany. So big were these trees that they had their own eco-systems, orchids, bromeliads, ferns and mosses adorning the upper branches creating beautiful hanging gardens. Vines invaded the trees, binding trunk and branch together to resemble massive serpents. These vines were capable of holding large amounts of good drinking water, and they also helped to stabilize the forest. Above the canopy in the sunlight there was a completely different ecology where monkeys, birds and insects thrived that never visited the jungle floor and would most likely have died if they had done so for any length of time. They live in their own warm sun-drenched world with a ready supply of food. Up there sound travels well and they are able to communicate with each other over great distances. Distress calls work well there too, unlike the jungle floor where sound is absorbed. They do have their own enemies, as snakes, hawks and eagles patrol the canopy constantly.

The empress cicada, a magnificent insect whose wings span eight inches, was often heard but very rarely seen. This insect has the most beautiful wings and Victorian collectors would go to great lengths to get hold of them, using dust shot fired from a shotgun. The atlas moth, the biggest in the world with a wing span of ten inches, was quite common and like most moths came out at night attracted to light; just imagine trying to read with one fluttering around your kerosene lamp.

At the base of those giant trees huge buttresses are formed, resembling space rocket fins. Many of the buttresses fused into each other forming natural wooden pools, some of which contained small fish belonging to the carp family which were the most delicious fish I've ever eaten, wrapped in leaves placed in a mess-tin and steamed for a few minutes over a solid fuel tablet; delicious, and very easy to catch too. Dip your mess-tin into the water and in they go to investigate. It's not certain how these fish got into the tree pools, but most likely birds or animals introduced them, as wading in rivers they would pick up the sticky eggs on fur or feather only to have them washed off in the pools whilst drinking or bathing. The sad thing is, sometimes it was necessary to blow up these magnificent trees to make a DZ (dropping zone) and create a large enough clearing in the canopy so as to be visible from the air by the supply plane. We used cordite and plastic explosive to cut and blast the tree into the planned direction of fall. A large cross of shiny white cloth was spread out in the middle of the clearing to aid visual contact. It wasn't safe to hang around in a DZ for obvious reasons, especially as the blasting down of the trees could have been heard for a great distance. The time while we waited for the drop was spent looking and listening at the periphery, sometimes for a whole day. Radio communications were hit and miss in the jungle, mostly miss, as there was no solid-state integrated transistor circuitry in those days.

The CT (communist terrorists) were the most amazing enemy and they deserve a mention, having been in the jungle for many years. They died mainly as a result of their own misfortunes rather than our superior weaponry and organisation, and it wasn't clear why they were still fighting. They had weapons so rusty, misaligned, patched and tied together with split bamboo that it would have been better if they had hit us with them rather than try to fire them at us. The problem was, most fatalities were caused by their weapons exploding in their faces as a result of not having the proper ammo, or bullets jamming in the rusty barrel. Nevertheless, they were a formidable foe and their technique of jungle survival was second to none.

We often came across their campsites, just a couple of atap branches fixed up over a bed of leaves and that was it. We never found where they may have made a fire, if they ever did. This enemy could disappear without a trace, and that can be surprisingly hard to do in the jungle, especially without making a noise. One method they used that we later discovered was to bury themselves in the watery bogs and hold on to submerged tree roots. The dark brown colour of the water and the green slime made it impossible to see them and they would breath through a hollow section of bamboo.

Pygmies, or aborigines, as we called them, lived deep in

the rain forest; their average height was about four-foot six inch and that's for a big adult. They used ten-foot long blowpipes and foot-long darts coated with poison taken from rubbing the dart in the slime of the tree frog's back. They hunted with deadly accuracy and could bring down a monkey from a great height. They were a friendly lot if they got to know you, and if we were passing through their kampong (village) they would bring out all their treasures to show us. One guy had a shotgun all stripped down and laid out on a piece of cloth, and he sat cross-legged in front of it with a grin like a piano keyboard, complete with the black keys. Others had various artifacts which they treasured, and all were on show. The females were naked but for a small skirt usually made of grass. They gave us information on the CTs' movements for a few cigarettes, and they gave the same information about us to the CTs. I have often wondered what they got from them.

My mate caught something very nasty during a patrol, but luckily he managed to get back to the platoon base camp. He was the section commander and was laid up in his hammock, his entire skin surface covered in blisters similar to nettle rash. He was either too hot or too cold, and he became quite delirious, not knowing who he was or where he was. The MO (medical orderly) wasn't much help, as he himself was supporting a huge face and an enormous appendage, having been bitten on the nose. The night before he had slept on the ground and a snake had slid under his poncho and cuddled up to him. At some time, he must have disturbed it and it bit him on the nose, so thank God it was a non-poisonous one. The section commander didn't respond to any of the usual treatments like castellanies paint, which was more like antifouling paint for a boat than a medical treatment. It was assumed he had scrub typhus – nobody knew what scrub typhus was, but his symptoms nearly corresponded to the diagnostic found in the book of tropical diseases. Anyway, after two or three days he shook it off and was soon back to his old bull-shitty ways. The MO's nose continued to grow and eventually he was shipped out and we never saw him again. The replacement MO had a naturally large nose and we all laughed when we saw him, but he couldn't see the funny side of it at all.

Chapter 6

Time off

~~~~~~

As a relief from jungle life, a colleague and I were dispatched to Singapore to take charge of a sports field and swimming pool complex shared by the RAF and their families. We were an advance party and the battalion were to follow and move into the barracks. You had to have time out of the jungle for the sake of sanity. It was in the grounds of the famous Salarang barracks, where the Japanese held their British and Commonwealth prisoners. The concrete three-storey building was riddled with bullet holes. God knows what went on here as everywhere you looked there were bullet holes.

Our accommodation was an isolated wood and asbestos

prefab-type shed at the side of an airstrip well away from the barracks, and it had a sink, toilet and proper beds with clean sheets. Oh, what luxury we thought. But all that glitters is not gold, and in the morning the crisp white sheets were speckled with blood. We could not understand it, as there were no bites on our bodies, but every morning was the same. The beds were stripped and mattresses beaten and all windows were closed at night, but whatever we did made no difference, blood would be on the sheets again in the morning. It was agreed there must be something in the mattresses. I discarded my mattress and slept on just a sheet on the metal springs, but in the morning it was worse.

"That's it," I said. The bed was taken outside and inspected in great detail, and to our amazement the small springs supporting the wire base were packed with bed bugs, all fat with blood. A large bonfire was made and the metal beds springs slowly passed through, and the smell of cooking bed bugs was actually quite nice. The problem was solved and we made a special trip to the Britannia Hotel in Singapore to celebrate our victory over the bed bugs.

I really enjoyed this job and the time I spent at this posting. Being a physical training instructor meant I was on hand at the swimming pool where I could meet the opposite sex. They were mainly wives from the RAF station, but they had daughters and I got to know some of them. Being so long away from females and the outside world I had sort of lost the knack of communication, apart from shouting orders to men. I had a small office, more like a room attached to the main building, where I could look out on whatever was going on in and around the pool, and it also looked over the men's and women's dressing room facilities.

One particular day the pool was quite busy, and I noticed an unusual amount of men going into the dressing room, then after a short time coming out still fully dressed. It did not make sense, so off I went to investigate. "What the hell are you doing, get out all of you!" I shouted. In the dividing wall between the men and women's quarters, a wooden knot had fallen out exposing a nice little hole in the wall, small enough to go unnoticed. Of course I had a quick look just to see what could be seen, but they had all left. The room was closed and I got the wall fixed.

On several occasions, I was invited to visit the RAF social club inside the actual station complex, which meant passing close to a row of fantastic, beautiful, streamlined jet fighters. It was a bit of a snobby place, but I did meet some very nice and interesting people who I got on with very well.

I was walking down a main street in Singapore when I came across a woman who had broken the heel of one of her high heel shoes and was having difficulty walking. I stopped and asked if I could be of any help. "Oh yes, if I could have your arm to support me, I would be very grateful," she said in perfect English. She was a beautiful woman and I helped her home. She lived in a substantial building with a polished brass dentist's sign on the building near the door. She thanked me very much and said she would like to see me again if that was possible.

"Well yes, that would be very nice" I said, handing her the broken heel. "There's a film on at the cinema called Ben Hur, it's in the new Technicolor, would you like to see it?"

"Oh, I would love to see it," she said.

"Meet you outside the cinema then at seven."

"Ok" she said, and went into the building with a little wave goodnight.

I met her the next night and we went into the cinema foyer. There were lots of people there waiting to go into the theatre and strangely enough they all seemed to be looking at us. Some would look, turn their heads and giggle at each other, and some people just giggled outright. At first I thought it was because I was foreign, but when I looked around there were lots of foreigners and they didn't get a single glance. It was ether me or the girl they were interested in. Someone once said to me I looked a bit like Charlton Heston, and I wondered for a moment if they might think I was him, the star in the film – of course we can all dream.

I spent two or three evenings with her, and we walked the town but always ended up in the city's cemetery, which is understandable as there were no other people in there, apart from the residents of course. We attempted lovemaking, but it all seemed to be a bit one sided. I wasn't that experienced myself but I was getting quite curious, as things didn't seem to add up.

To cut a long story short, this beautiful woman was a transvestite, and a very good one too. Some people would say surely you must have known, but I'm telling you it was not that simple. I'm not going to tell you how I found out, but she turned out to be quite a handful. Oh and she still has my camera, one of those bellows types.

There's a place in Malaya called the Cameron Highlands. It's quite a magical place with a unique atmosphere and a climate all of its own, hot during the day and cold enough at night to put goosebumps on the hardiest of legs. In this mountainous region everything was larger than life and the insects were enormous. There were rare but nevertheless shy tigers, or they could have been clouded leopards – it was hard to say as I never got a really good look at them. They lived in the dense vegetation that rolled up into the clouds and occasionally appeared at the edge of the jungle like ghosts, and on the second blink of the eye they were gone. It was easy to imagine that dinosaurs lived there. Massive tree ferns, living fossils and descendants from the Jurassic period, dominated the landscape. They were exactly the same as the fossils I used to see running along the roof of the coal seam when I was down the mine. To get there involved hours of zigzagging, bone-shaking, vomit-throwing, eyeball-rolling journey by Land Rover up the mountainside on a perilous dust track with sheer drop-offs, up through clouds into the thin atmosphere. It could have been another world.

Because this place was so high and the air so rarefied, a hospital for the treatment of TB (tuberculosis) a bacterial lung disease, had been built. I was posted there to introduce remedial physical training to the patients, most of whom were Gurkhas. On arriving I was given a couple of weeks to acclimatise as the air was so thin, and I made friends with a Chinese chap called Kim who was the camp signal and radio operator. He too was interested in collecting insects, and we made many a foray into the jungle at night armed only with flashlights and a stick, turning over rotting logs looking for the two-inch long rhino beetle and stag beetles. There was another beetle we often came across which was about two inches long with very long antennae and amazingly strong jaws. It could bite a matchstick in two with ease.

At the end of my two weeks' rest it was time to start work. I reported to the hospital and met the patients, about thirty Gurkhas all bouncing up and down. Oh, I thought, they look quite fit, so we set off on a two-mile run. Knowing Gurkhas are used to hilly country, I chose the hardest course. After about a mile they were showing some very odd symptoms, so I was forced to cut short the run and return them to the hospital. The matron was waiting with hands on hips as I delivered a heap of gasping, retching, kneeling bodies, and she shook her fist under my nose. I honestly thought she was going to hit me, and she banned me from the hospital grounds there and then.

I was reported to my superior officer, who as it turned out was a female major, with an office in a small flimsy wooden hut built on a platform about two feet off the ground. I reported dressed in my best uniform, marched in and came to a very smart, very heavy attention on the thin wooden floor. Her desk hovered momentarily and its contents were thrown to the floor. Not knowing how to address a female rank, I called her missus. That didn't go down very well at all. She pulled her desk back into place and reminded me to address her as ma'am and then had me pick up her pen and papers.

She told me I had just undone months of treatment and was to stay away from the hospital and busy myself elsewhere, and for six months that's exactly what I did. I spent a lot of time in the kampong, a local small village, with Kim, who introduced me to some wonderful Chinese food. He also introduced me to a small restaurant owner who showed me his three-inch long rhino beetle, just the kind of thing we were looking for. I really got a feel for this place.

Through Kim I met a Malay Indian called Hasmid, who was the camp accountant, and his Chinese wife, and they took a shine to me and asked if I would like to accompany them on a tour north towards the Thai border and Penang Island with all expenses paid. I got the necessary permission from my commanding officer, the ma'am, who gave me a sideways smile and said "Of course you can, corporal", and I dressed as a civilian to go out of the area. It was like an eating holiday with everything paid for. I ate everything from frogs' legs and snakes to things I've never seen before and glazed eyeballs.

One time in a small open-air restaurant with just three tables, in a very small village with chickens and dogs running around our feet, I thought I'd reached my limit in culinary experience. Delivered to the table was a huge silver-looking dish with a high domed lid which seemed totally out of context, given the bare well-trodden earth beneath our feet. In fact the ground was so uneven that one leg of the table was sitting on an empty turtle shell and the other leg rested on a discarded flip-flop. With great pride and a lot of head nodding it was presented to the centre of the table. Village onlookers, certainly not used to seeing a white person attending their little eating place, moved closer and gathered around. I was a little uneasy to say the least, and had never had an audience watching me eat before.

The dish bearer had a wide smile with just one enormous tooth in the centre top part of his mouth, which still showed even when his mouth was closed. The lid was removed with great ceremony, and a murmur rippled through the crowd. I was looking at a raw chicken complete with its red head, goose flesh and fluffy feather stubs. I looked around and everyone was nodding approval as the waiter backed away carrying the lid.

Hasmid saw my concern and my dropped jaw, and laughed. He assured me it was cooked but in a different way. He took the legs, shook them and the whole bird just fell out of its skin. He told me the chicken had been marinaded in herbs and spices for a long time and then steamed just before serving. I must admit it was delicious. I thought that was the main meal, but Hasmid ordered Indian-style food, which was excellent, and his Chinese wife chose her native food, Cantonese and from other regions of her country.

I tried the Chinese meat consommé and wow, what an amazing taste from something that looked just like water! I have been to some very posh restaurants in my time, but the food here really took some beating. Not the kind of food you get from the local takeaway. I must admit it was a truly wonderful experience.

Hasmid's wife said, "While we are in the area why don't we visit the snake temple?"

"What a good idea" Kim said, and I added, "I would love to see it," so off we went. It was at a place called Sungai Kluang Penang and I must admit I was a little sceptical as to what we were going to see. It turned out to be beyond belief. There was a temple with lots of incense sticks burning throughout and it was full of snakes. They were everywhere, many different kinds and were even in the bushes outside the temple. No one knows why they congregated at this place as there were no keepers or anyone looking after them and they were free to come and go as they pleased. Quite amazing! I had my photo taken with one of the snakes in a bush at the side of me. I have since heard it's a lot more commercial now. Visiting a country with someone who can speak the language is fantastic, as you really get to know the local traditions and customs. I was away for five days and I must have put on weight. In those days I really did have a six-pack, unlike today, now I have a belly more like a keg.

Back at the camp a friend John, who was a chef at the hospital, and I were on a cross-country run when we came across a field full of pineapples. "Wow, let's get in there" I said. It was a blistering hot day and we thought a drink of pineapple juice would be just the trick. With the aid of a penknife we set about cutting into them. They weren't quite ripe and were very hard but tasted rather good, so we ate what we needed and set off back to camp.

A little while later our lips began to swell and we could not bear our tongues to touch anywhere in the mouth – even breathing was painful. We were walking around with our mouths wide open and the tongue centred in the middle. It was so embarrassing, as we could not speak to tell people why we were like this. The condition lasted for about two hours. Apparently, the acid in the pineapple was so strong it had burnt the inside of our mouths and made it extremely sensitive. I look at pineapples in a different light these days and they have to be ripe to the point of almost rotten for my liking.

Word got around, I don't know how, that I was at a loose end, and a tea planter of British nationality who had a plantation on the lower slopes approached me and asked if I would guard his house for a week. He said he had spoken to the commanding officer and had got permission to ask me. His house was in a very remote area and he and his family had to go to Kuala Lumpur. I got permission from the camp commandant to draw my SLR (self-loading rifle) and two magazines of 7.62 ammo. I dressed as a civilian and tried to look like a tea planter, complete with a floppy white hat, but I was ever mindful that I was still on active service and terrorists could strike at any time or place, though it might have been too cold at night for living out in the open and access is limited to this part of the country, so it was less likely that they would be here.

We set off in his Land Rover and the journey took the best part of the day. Going down the mountain, the change of temperature caused condensation to form on the Land Rover's body and windscreen. We arrived at his house to find a beautiful white colonial-type place with a veranda all around draped with colourful exotic flowering vines, overlooking rolling hills of tea plants that stretched further than the eye could see. This place must have been in their family for generations. Exquisitely-carved dark wood furniture was scattered throughout the house, and there were antiques and treasures everywhere. It's no wonder he needed an armed guard looking after the place.

I was shown to my room, a good choice as I could see most of the surrounding area and especially the access road to the house. I settled in and was soon invited down to dinner, where I met the rest of his family, his wife, daughter and young son. We had roast wild pig, roast spuds and Yorkshire pudding, and it was fantastic. I immediately fell in love with his beautiful daughter, who had long raven hair and a figure to die for. Each time she looked up from her meal she caught me looking at her and I got some funny sideways glances from her younger brother.

After dinner we all sat around telling stories. I did a couple of so-called magic tricks and that made the young lad warm to me a little, but the daughter was very shy and kept her distance. I never really got to know her, and when she left early the next morning I wondered if I would see her again.

The next day, after the family had left, I did some exploring in my new role as a tea planter. I wandered down the hillside to the wooden huts where the women tea pickers, dressed in brightly-coloured saris and carrying baskets almost as big as themselves, emptied their tea plant leaves onto the drying tables. The manager came up, bowed politely and introduced himself. He was very dark and of Indian origin, but he spoke good English. At first he thought I was a new boss, but I told him the only thing I knew about tea was drinking it. He showed me around the place, and the smell of tea was overwhelming. The women working there had to walk for miles and some of them had babies slung on their fronts as well as baskets on their backs. And I never even got offered a cup of tea!

It was an interesting week. I opened a cupboard and found it contained just about every type of tea in the world. There was not much to do, and it was very quiet during the day and deadly quiet at night apart from something running around in the attic. I could have shot a wild pig that was rooting in the garden, but then I thought there would be too much for me to eat, and I would have to explain why I was a round short when I handed in my weapon and ammo, so decided against it. I made meals from lots of goodies the tea planter's wife had left for me and there was a massive bow-fronted American-type freezer containing various types of meat, so I was well cared for. I read the whole of Grimm's Fairy Tales, as it was the only book I could find there, and if any other books had been available I would have read them, anything. It was the longest week I've ever spent.

When the family returned their beautiful daughter was not with them; I think she must have gone back to the UK for her education.

Their return meant it was time for me to head back to the hospital camp and hand in my rifle and ammo. They thanked me and said they would love to have spent more time with me but because we were living in different worlds, they being civilian and me in the army, sadly it was unlikely that we would meet again.

My time at the hospital complex was just about over, so I had to return to my regiment. I had hardly settled in when I was told that the Royal Navy was offering to take a small contingent of men from our battalion to go on board a frigate, the HMS *Belfast* bound for the South China Sea, and take part in an exercise in exchange for a similar group of naval personnel who would be allowed to experience life in the jungle. I thought it was a great idea. My name was put forward along with five others.

We boarded the *Belfast* at Singapore and set sail for the South China Sea. What a fantastic, formidable ship she was, it made me so proud to be aboard her. Life as a sailor was completely different from what we were used to, and even the rum ration was different. In the jungle we were only allowed a small measure, which we had to drink straight down, and it left us gasping for breath and unable to speak. On board we got a decent amount in a half-pint glass which was topped up with water and we could drink it whenever we liked, which seemed far more civilized.

When we arrived at the training area, I could see there were other ships in the vicinity. There was a floating target in the distance and the guns were manned. They were firing 40mm ammo and soon destroyed the target. We were allowed to go to most areas of the ship, and after the firing practice I was shown how to aim the gun, and I can tell you, it's not easy. I sat on it and looked through the sights. There appeared to be two floating rings which I had to line up so that only one ring was visible. All that together with the movement of the ship – bonkers! Another target they used was a sleeve being towed by a small airplane, with the ship firing at it with tracer shells. How mad is that and was there a real pilot flying the plane? I don't know, I assume there must have been.

I was on a lower deck on my way to my cabin when there was a massive explosion that lifted me up, or perhaps it was my reflexes – anyway it put me on my back. I couldn't see anything or hear anything and there were a lot of flashing lights in my head. I didn't know which way was up or down. Gradually my sight returned, but not my hearing. When I tried to stand up, I just rolled over and managed to sit with my back to a bulkhead. One of the crew saw me, came over and dragged me well away from the area. I couldn't walk because I had no balance. The guy knew this and that was why he didn't try to get me on my feet. "You must have been under the six-inch gun turret when they fired it," he said. He was joined by another guy and they got me back to my cabin. The other guy said it would be around two hours before I would be anything like normal and they went away.

Soon after the first guy returned with a cup of tea and a chocolate biscuit. The guys were right, it was about two hours before I could get about. The MO had a quick look at me and asked if I had any bleeding from the ears. "No," I said and he gave me the all clear. Later I was on the gun deck when they fired the same massive gun and there was no problem, but I did suffer from hearing loss in later years.

I must admit I quite liked life onboard ship and was sad when it was time to leave. I remember when I was called up I had had the option of joining the Army or Navy; for the Navy you had to sign on for twenty-two years minimum, which was too long for me, so Army it was.

My flight home was on a BOAC domestic airline with turbo-prop engines and my mate Vic and I were the only two service personnel on board. We stopped at Karachi in Pakistan, and maybe somewhere else, I can't remember, but the last stop before the UK was Athens. As we would be flying over neutral countries we had to be in civilian clothes and not representing the British Army. What we did would be absolutely out of the question nowadays, and we would probably be shot on sight. We arrived at London airport dressed in grey double-breasted suits. Mine hung on me like a curtain, the trousers came halfway up my khaki socks showing my shiny black army boots, the fly on my trousers came down to my knees and we were carrying our rifles over our shoulders with our khaki kit bags. We looked like something out of a gangster movie. The suits, shirts and ties were borrowed from the RAF base in Singapore and we had to hand them in to a depot somewhere in London. It was a good thing the taxi driver knew where it was. We then had to don our Army uniforms and get back to our barracks in order to hand in our firearms. The rifle was our own personal weapon, which we were responsible for though we did not have any ammo or magazines.

I went through customs first and said I had nothing to declare. My travelling companion was next and the customs officer asked him the same question. He said, "same as him" meaning me, and he came straight through. I found out later he had four 'Hong Kong bibles' (porn books) in his kitbag. That sort of thing was taken very seriously in those days.

Chapter 7

Back home

~~~~~

It was so nice to get back home after three years, though my sisters cried because they said I talked posh and with a funny accent. Next day my brother Rex said he had discovered a new Blue John mine, which is a beautiful purple crystal, in the Derbyshire hills and he wanted me to take a look at it with him. It turned out to be an abandoned lead mine used for mining galena, lead ore. We set off quite early the next day with a flask of tea and some sandwiches, and I found that the entrance wasn't much bigger than a foxhole. We lit our carbide lamps, also known as acetylene gas lamps, which use the reaction between calcium carbide and water. The entrance opened out into a cave and we travelled along it until it became several passages going off in different directions. "This is the one," he said. Rex had a one-piece boiler suit on and I had a corduroy jacket and pants, as none of my old clothes fitted me anymore.

He got down and disappeared into the tunnel, leaving me to follow him. It started off quite wide and gradually became narrower and narrower until it was getting to be a bit of a squeeze, so I was expecting a cavernous space at the end. We were on our knees and elbows when Rex yelled "That's it, it's a dead-end Nip [that's what he called me], start going back!" As I set about crawling backwards my jacket started rolling up over my back and jammed me solid. The next thing I knew Rex's boots were hitting me in the face. "Stop!" I shouted, "I'm bloody jammed!"

Claustrophobia started nagging at my brain, and I knew I had to control it. "Go forward" I said. It was a good thing he kept his cool and carried on going forward until I had unravelled my coat. I managed to get hold of my side jacket pockets and pull the coat tight over my back. Inch by inch I eased myself backwards. Then...

"Bollocks."

"What's up?" Rex shouted through an opening in his legs.

"I've knocked my lamp over and it's gone out," I replied. Then I noticed a strong smell of rotten eggs. "Oh my god, have you bloody farted?" I shouted.

"No, you silly bugger, it's the gas from the lamp," said Rex's arse. All I could see now was a glow of light coming from my brother's backside – well, I always thought the sun shone out of his bottom. We carried on inching our way backwards for what seemed like hours. Each time I gained some space I would tell him to come back about a foot, but he still managed to kick me in the face with his boots several times.

Eventually the tunnel widened and we made it back to the cave entrance. I had skinned both my elbows, had a cut on my nose and the leather patches on my jacket sleeves had worn through.

"What was that all about?" I enquired.

"Oh it was a tunnel I hadn't done," he said. We used to explore lead mines and Blue John mines before I was in the army.

"Well you very nearly killed us both. Did anybody know we were coming here?"

"No, but I said we were coming to Derbyshire."

"OK, that narrows it down a bit."

Arriving home there was a huge banner across the house: WELCOME HOME DAVE.

"What the fuck?" I turned to Rex, who had a big smile on his face. "So that's what this was all about, to get me out of the way, well you very nearly succeeded."

I told my mum how he had nearly killed me, in a joking manner of course, and she wagged a finger at him and said "You're not too big to come over my knee, my lad".

Most of the family were there and we all had a great homecoming party, but I reminded myself I only had a couple of weeks leave before returning to barracks.

We were posted to a training camp at Warcop in Cumbria, a well out of the way place miles from anywhere. We were to train up ready for our next commitment. It wasn't a bad place at all, a bit boring, lots of rifle practice. I swapped my white shorts and vest, tropical PT gear, for warmer black slacks and a red and black striped jumper. I did quite a lot of fishing, as there was a beautiful river close by. I caught grayling, trout and eels and one evening I took a large, live eel back to camp to cook, as they are supposed to be good eating. It was extremely slippery. The only way you can prepare them is to put them on sheets of newspaper, which stops them sliding all over the place, and this worked very well. I cut the eel into two-inch lengths and they were still wriggling about, so I put them into the frying pan and they were getting nice and brown but they were still moving. They did not seem to stop moving right up until they were getting burnt. They were very tasty but eating them without thinking they were still moving was harder to do than I thought. I reminded myself I had eaten far worse, but only one other guy would risk eating it.

One weekend, a group of us decided to head for the nearest pub, which was in a town called Appleby, a really lovely little town just off the A66, but not having transport we had to thumb a lift. We split up into twos to give us more chance of success. Eventually we all got into town and met up in the pub. As the night wore on it was all getting a bit too boisterous, so my mate and I went into a small back room where there was a piano. I was playing something when the rest of the gang burst in. They were very loud and quite drunk, and one guy stood on a chair and pissed into the back of the piano.

"That's it, I'm off" I said, and walked out. My mate followed and we went to another pub. We had to be back at the camp guardhouse by 2359 hours, but we could not get a lift. I didn't know how the rest of the guys were getting back, but we were getting short of time.

My mate suggested we borrow a small motorbike that was leaning against a wall inside an open yard. We tried to start it but we couldn't – of course you had to have a key. With all the fuss and palaver someone must have phoned the police. A young police officer drove up and we ran, but unfortunately, he caught Dennis, my mate, who fell over. The police officer was driving up and down the road looking for me so I gave myself up, got in the car and we were driven to the police station. We were only doing what we had been trained to do at all costs and whatever it took to get back to camp. The copper gave us a lift back to camp, but we still had a lot of explaining to do.

After about a week we were to appear in the local courthouse charged with attempted theft. The officer representing us from our battalion said we had an exemplary service record and we were just showing high spirits, having just returned from a three-year active service tour in the Far East. But of course, it was no excuse and we were fined thirty shillings each, that's £1.50 pence.

The next case was a giant of a man, both upward and sideways, a soldier like us but not from our battalion, and he was involved in a similar case to ours as he had stolen a child's pushbike and the bike in question was in court. The judge, a woman of a bonny nature, couldn't understand how he could possibly ride such a small bike, which was for a seven or eight-year-old child and she would like to see how it was possible. The bike was handed to the giant for a demonstration, and when he sat on the bike it almost disappeared from view. The courtroom erupted in laughter and even the judge turned her head to hide her face. He was fined thirty shillings, the same as us.

On a weekend off from duty, a fellow corporal and I went to Appleby to fish the beautiful River Eden. We needed to buy some more fishing tackle from the local shop, and once fully equipped we set off to fish the river, which runs through the town. We were hoping to catch some grayling, a beautiful fish with a very large dorsal fin, which is also nice to eat.

We were not doing very well at all. My mate cast his line and it snagged on a bush over the other side of the river. He couldn't free it, so he aligned his fishing rod with the branch on which he was snagged and started winding in his reel. The line was getting tighter and tighter and something had to give. I was watching out of interest. His float was made from a porcupine quill the same as mine, and was about ten inches long.

Suddenly the hook gave way and the porcupine float flew straight at him like an arrow from a bow. It went through his pants and hit him in his penis. He threw his rod away and pulled the quill out very quickly. I have never seen so much blood – it was flooding out from the bottom of his trousers, I ran to the nearest shop and told the shopkeeper to ring for an ambulance, which he did. I then told my mate to put his hand in his pants and hold himself as tight as he could to try and stop the flow, as I honestly thought he would bleed to death. The ambulance arrived and rushed him straight to hospital. I learnt a valuable lesson that day, as in the past I had done a very similar thing, but I guess I was lucky.

From this posting in Cumbria we were shipped to Aldershot in Hampshire. Why I'm not quite sure, but I did have a very large gymnasium at my disposal. Set in a huge field, it had a back room complete with a small kitchen and a bedroom, and officers would bring their platoons here for PT.

I had bought a scooter whilst I was at this posting, a Zundap Bella, Italian, a big heavy thing that I used to travel to Nottingham at the weekends so I could see my family. When I was coming back from one such trip overnight during the winter I hit a patch of black ice, skidded across the road and into a ditch, smashing my wonderful windscreen and receiving cuts and bruises to my hands and legs. I got the scooter back on the road and continued my journey, but without the windscreen and with no goggles, it was very painful and bitterly cold with my eyes streaming water so badly I could hardly see, so it was a slow ride.

When I arrived at the gym there was an officer and about thirty men jumping around waiting for PT class. I pulled myself together and ordered them to run around the field non-stop three times, which gave me time to get changed into my PT gear and put a plaster on my cut hand.

My next posting was to Northern Ireland. This was before the Troubles, and it was more of a hanging-out posting where we trained and basically kept fit. One day, as a change from the norm, I decided to take the men on a run around the village, dressed in their fatigue outfit instead of shorts and vest. We set off on a two-mile run through the village at the rear of the barracks. It was a beautiful day and there were lots of people about. We were a squad of about thirty men in three ranks, two of the ranks were running on the road and the other rank on the pavement so we didn't take up too much space. We were passing a school building, and outside they had a metal railing which stood about four feet six inches high and about twenty feet long situated at the edge of the road, designed to stop children from running straight into the road when they poured out of school.

I was at the rear of the squad dressed in my spotless white PT gear; we were nearing the end of the run when I was suddenly bowled over in great pain. I could hardly breathe, and I was hanging over the school barrier fighting for my breath. I was certain I had broken a rib or something. The men had run either side of the railing, but I hadn't seen it and ran into it at full force whilst looking elsewhere, most likely at a girl.

The squad was totally unaware as to what had happened and were blindly running on, and it was impossible for me to catch them up or even shout any commands. Then a corporal at the rear of the squad happened to turn around and see me bent double trying to walk, so he took command of the squad and halted them. With some help from the men I was able to get back to the barracks. It turned out I had cracked my sternum (breastbone) and it affected certain abilities of mine for years.

One of our keeping fit exercises was a 48-hour route march in the Mountains of Mourne with all our equipment in a trailer towed behind a Land Rover. We were well into the mountains when we were hit by a violent snowstorm. It struck without warning and was relentless, so we had to stop and huddle together as we could not see a bloody thing. When the snow hit us it turned to ice. The sheep had about two feet of snow on their backs and when they fell over, they couldn't get back up as it was frozen to their backs, making them top heavy. The road became a dangerous place to be as it was narrow and had dense hedgerows on both sides, so it filled with snow in minutes and the Land Rover was completely covered, along with all our camping gear and food. Conditions were worsening by the minute, but luckily, we were near a farm which had a barn, so we moved in.

What followed was unbelievable. In a short time we were experiencing ice blizzards and even in the barn our trousers froze until they were as stiff as pipes. It was just as well that we were properly dressed with long johns, insulated trousers and long fur-lined parka jackets. I took two men to see if we could get into the trailer, and we managed to get to it through the thick snow but found the rope tying the cover down was frozen solid with ice and it was impossible to undo the knots.

By the time I got back the officer was talking to the farmer, who told him we had to get out because he wanted to put his sheep in. "Where the hell can we go?" I heard him say. The farmer turned his back on him saying "I don't know" and walked off. The only other place nearby was the church, so the lieutenant took the platoon and headed for the church. I stayed back to make sure there were no cigarette ends left smouldering anywhere. When I arrived at the church the men had already taken their wet clothing off and some of it was draped over the altar and elsewhere - better not mention where. I told the men to remove their gear and hang it on the back of the pews. The lieutenant was in the back room organising lighting the boiler when the padre burst into the church from the back door and ordered us out immediately. He said we had committed mortal sin on the Roman Catholic Church. With this the lieutenant raised his voice and said "What do you mean, most of these soldiers are Roman Catholic, for God's sake!"

"That's beside the point" the padre ranted. "There's a farm just up the road, he is more suited to cater for your kind." He stormed around mumbling under his breath till we were outside and ready to leave, then he slammed the door shut behind us with the sound of a heavy bolt being rammed home. The road to our next place was quite clear of snow as it ran in a different direction, so the snow was blowing along it and was not being trapped by the hedges causing it to drift. It was quite dark, but because of the snow we could at least see where we were going.

When we reached the farmhouse, there was a chap waiting at the door. He welcomed us into his huge kitchen, which was lovely and warm. It had a range running the whole length of the kitchen with a large peat-burning stove in the middle. At both sides of the stove were piles of peat in various stages of drying, so there was always dry peat ready for the stove. This guy really looked after us. He gave us a fantastic meat stew with homemade bread. We helped with all chores and did whatever he wanted us to do. Then we all bedded down on whatever available space we could find in the kitchen and were so happy to do so, given the weather outside.

The radio operator finally got communication with the rest of the company and a meeting place was organised. The farmer was rewarded for his hospitality and we set off to regroup at a pre-arranged map reference. We had been away for seven days. My family told me they had phoned the battalion HQ daily, and they had said there was no word as to where we were or when we would be back. It made the headlines on the BBC News reporting a company of soldiers lost in the Mourne Mountains, which had really worried our families. Later we heard that there had been some casualties among older people, and that was why the helicopters were flying about all over the place. The Land Rover was recovered, still full of all our gear but we never got to ride in it, as we had to walk out.

At this posting we were on what was known as the strategic reserve, which meant we were available to be posted anywhere in the world, and towards the latter end of my service we were sent to Tripoli, the capital of Libya, to get some desert training under our belts. This was before we had even heard of Muammar Gaddafi, who seized power in a military coup in 1969. This was a massive exercise involving the RAF and other forces.

A desert base camp was set up and latrines were dug in the desert sand. They consisted of two planks of wood stretched over a very deep trench and in the middle was a bottomless box on which you sat and that was it, no privacy at all. One night after a drinking session an Irish guy fell into the trench after attempting to walk the planks to the bog. He was there all night, as nobody could hear him shouting because the bog was too far from camp and the trench was too deep to climb out of. He was in a terrible state when discovered in the morning half buried in sand and crying, asking for his mum. He was shipped back to the UK for some reason or other.

After about a week it was time to play soldiers, so we headed out into the desert. There was just one hill for miles around, and that's where me and another chap were posted, right on the very top. The first thing we did was dig a hole about two feet deep for our water bottles to try and keep them as cool as possible. From our vantage point we could see all the other guys spread out digging trenches, so we dug our trench and were sitting in it wondering what the next move would be. It has to be said on this kind of exercise there was a lot of sitting around waiting.

It was unbelievably hot and the sun was still climbing when suddenly there was an ear-shattering sound; a jet plane had come out of the sun, flying so low we could smell the hot metallic exhaust fumes as it passed over us at tremendous speed. The pilot had dropped a bag of white flour which burst on contact with the ground, covering everything in the white stuff, including us. That was it, we were out of the exercise, as we were classed as dead by the officials, so we made our way back to the camp. While we were in this desert, it rained not just a drop but a torrential downpour for most of a day and the whole camp was flooded. The Arabs were catching it and storing it in whatever containers they could find. For us it was a problem, as it brought the small sandy-coloured scorpions out from their burrows, the deadly poisonous ones which should be treated with great care, so sleeping bags and boots had to be checked over before use. Another unforeseen aspect was fleas brought into camp by the guys riding camels – they seemed to be lathered in them.

Our next posting was Cyprus, where Archbishop Makarios was doing his thing. We were to man what they called the thin green line, which was a no man's land between the Turkish and Greek Cypriots, it was all over the news back in the UK. The Greeks welcomed us with open arms at first and offered us their local brandy, but soon they accused us of favouring the Turks and turned against us – just like that. Both sides shot over our heads. They could shoot at us, but we couldn't shoot back at them. We sat in a trench topped with sandbags, bullets cracking over our heads. Now and again we would be rained on by sand when they had hit the sand bags, and we couldn't do a darn thing about it.

One time we had to go out into the countryside to rescue a Turkish family, a man, woman and two children, who had been pinned down by a machine gun by Greek Cypriots on the flat roof of a two-storey building. They were in a small wooden shack. The bottom planks of the wall had been smashed out to allow an arm to reach out and gather whatever plants and even grass they could reach to eat, so the ground all around the shack was bare of vegetation. They must have done this at night. A chicken run and hut were full of dead birds, having been shot to pieces along with a tethered goat, and there was a terrible stink about the place. They were clearly suffering from starvation, and it was a miracle the two children were still alive.

We boldly marched in, rifles at the ready and set up a GPMG (general purpose machine gun), the new 7.62mm version, on a bipod trained at the Greek position as a show of force. This gun can lay down a tremendous number of rounds per minute and is so concentrated it can cut through solid concrete.

The officer, I and two other men walked up to the shack, and halfway the officer turned and shouted loudly so the Greek gunmen could hear, "If they fire a single round, take the fucking roof off". "Yes sir!" they shouted, and that gun could easily do just that. Of course, we would not open fire as it was not allowed, we were a peace-keeping force.

When the family saw us approaching with UN insignia on our uniforms they broke down and ran out to hug us. Judging by the smell and the general condition of the family they must have been there quite a long time. There was no movement whatsoever from the rooftop – the gun had simply disappeared. We escorted the Turks out of the area amidst a lot of angry screaming and abuse from the Greeks. There was an enormous crowd awaiting us when we delivered the family back to the Turkish quarter, though how they knew we were coming I'll never know. They were a poor people, but they offered us fruit and cigarettes by the handful, but we could not take anything as that would show we were taking sides. The Greeks accused us of that anyway.

Chapter 8

Civvy Street

~~~~~~

Throughout my Northern Ireland posting I had acquired an insatiable interest in electronics. I studied books and magazines and carried out small experiments with batteries, relays and stuff like that. This was a time when transistors were starting to appear in portable radios, and if you had a radio with seven transistors you had the dog's testicles of radios, though nowadays of course there are hundreds of transistors in portable radios. I would go to St George's Market in Belfast, where you could buy just about anything. I remember buying two transistors, OC71s, each in its small aluminium capsule with three wires sticking out, base, collector and emitter. I had no idea what to do with them or how they worked, but I had to have them and I was determined to learn. I dismantled old electrical equipment, learnt the colour code of resisters and capacitors, which were called condensers in those days.

This then was the start of my career when discharged from the army. I did manage to make a small crystal radio, cats' whiskers they were called, which only worked if I connected it to the outside iron sewer pipe which served as an aerial. I continued to study and experiment whenever I could.

My first job after leaving the army in 1964 was at Rediffusion, the television rental company, based in Nottingham. It was a great employer for taking on unqualified personnel and training them up, and I learnt so much. One of the guys who was teaching me said one day "What do you see when you look into the back of a television?"

"A mass of wires and valves," I said.

"Ahh, what you have to see are the sections," he said. "It's like a car, wheels, brakes, steering, engine, it's all made up of parts that make the whole thing a car. With a TV, you break it down into its separate circuits such as the line generator, sound circuits and vision, the scanning coil components and so on." That's what he taught me to do, and it all started to make sense. It was the time when 405 line TV was being replaced by 625 lines, and a separate workshop was set up and a team of engineers, under the control of a wonderful man called Ted, were assembled to carry out the job of converting the company's televisions to the new 625 line operation. I was one of the team. It was interesting work and soon I and other members of the team were converting TVs in people's houses. I stayed with this company and learnt the basic principles of TV servicing and lots more.

Some of my early experiments with TVs were not only insane but very dangerous. I remember I frightened my wife so much, unintentionally of course, that there were times when I thought she was about to pass out. We were living at my mum's house at the time and I was in the attic doing an experiment with the high-tension lead from a TV's high voltage transformer, the one that connects to the anode of the cathode ray tube. It has a voltage of about 20-25,000 volts but low current (by telling you this I am admitting how bonkers I was). I stood on a sheet of glass, which was the front of an old TV, in my bare feet, holding tight the extended wire of the transformer. I also had a tennis ball with me on the glass. If I held the wire loosely, I would get a shock. I charged up my body. The high static voltage attracted dust and fluff which flew to my feet and stuck there. My hair streamed upwards, giving off a blue aura and a strong smell of ozone. Just then my wife came upstairs and saw me, and she screamed and ran down shouting for my mum. I knew I would get a shock when I let go of the wire, so I had to discharge myself slowly, and I did this by bouncing the ball on and off the wall several times until it was safe to get off the glass. I knew it would be all right to get off the glass when the dust and fluff fell away from me. It was very difficult explaining exactly what I had been doing and I got a lot of very worried looks from my family. I could almost hear them thinking, do we need to call someone? The truth was I didn't quite know what I was doing myself.

But, time to move on. I worked for a few small independent TV rental firms, and one of these was a TV rental company specialising in coin-operated TVs which had a box on the back into which coins were inserted to get a certain amount of TV time. I was called out on one occasion to fix a TV, and the customer at this address turned out to be a guy who had bullied me at school. I looked at the back of the television and saw the black box had been smashed open. "What's happened here then?" I said.

"Oh, the bloody kid hit it with a shoe." The kid in question was a two-year-old. "You would need a big hammer to break quarter-inch thick Bakelite" I told him. "So where's the money gone?"

"Ah, well we haven't been using it" he said. I noticed a large empty gin bottle on the floor at the side of a chair. Yes, that's where the money's gone, I thought. I picked up the TV and took it straight to the van, and he followed me out shouting abuse. I don't think he recognised me, as I had changed a lot since school and could have made mincemeat of him now "The firm will be in touch with you" I said and drove off.

I saw an advert in the local paper for a TV engineer, basic pay of twenty pounds per week, which was twice what I was getting, so I applied and got the job. It was a bigger rental company and I found out that the wage was for a seven-day week, but anyway I gave it a go and soon got into it. They supplied me with a Minivan, which I thought was a bit on the small side considering the size of some of the televisions. On one occasion I went to repair a set in a house on a large housing estate. They were an old couple and their TV was a very small one. It had a fault which couldn't be fixed in their house so would have to go back to the workshop. I told them they could get a bigger one for the same amount of money, but no, they wanted this one back. The manager at the shop said "This bloody thing's not worth repairing".

"I know that" I said, "but they want this one back." After a few days I returned the set. During my journey I had to make an emergency stop for a cow that suddenly ran onto the road from an open gate. The small TV, because of its rounded shape, rolled around the van, became airborne and impaled itself on the bolt that protrudes from the wheel arch inside the van. The bolt had made a hole in the top of the set about two inches wide. Because I was quite close to the address, I went there to tell them what had happened. They welcomed me in and said they didn't mind at all because they put a lace mat over the set anyway. I switched on and the set worked perfectly. They said it was absolutely OK and were very happy with it. By the time I had got back to the shop they had phoned complaining about a massive hole in the top of the set, before I could explain to the manager what had happened. Like I say, you meet all sorts in this game.

Working seven days a week I had no time for my family, and it was getting quite tiresome. I decided to go self-employed as a TV repair engineer, and my job took me into people's homes. In Nottingham there is an area called The Meadows and I was called to a house on Crocus Street – what a beautiful-sounding address, I thought. The house was an old two or three-storey Victorian building, and the entrance was a pitch-black passage to a door at the far end. It was so dark I had to feel my way along the wall. The door was opened and I found myself looking into a massive room. I could not believe what I was seeing. A woman who was impeccably dressed and very well-spoken asked me in. There was a single track leading straight to the TV and it branched off to a small kitchen area. Either side of the track were piles of rubbish at least a foot high, and everything you could imagine was there. From the TV the track led to an open door, out of which a man came out. He just stood there, wearing a beautiful Fair Isle knitted jumper, which was far too small for his bulbous belly and I could see his hairy belly button. He had probably got it through his work, I thought. We got talking and he said he was a refuse collector with the council. What could I possibly say to that? I tried to think. I nearly said "Seems to me you bring your work home with you," but I didn't. They were nice enough people, and of course it's good to have such a diversity of folk, I think. On leaving I found myself wiping my feet on the mat outside the door.

I went into rich folks' homes and poor folks', and sometimes I did the repair for nothing. My busiest times were Christmas and when a long-running series was about to conclude, such as The Fugitive for instance, and my services were in great demand. Many times I was called out on Christmas Eve or New Year's Eve and found nothing wrong with their TV – all the customer wanted was company. There was usually a table full of food and drink, and I was invited to join the customer in a meal. When I was about to go they would say "Oh take some of this food with you, I can't eat it all on my own". With a lump in my throat I thought, how can you charge someone like that? It's no wonder I was driving a clapped-out ten-year-old van.

I remember on one occasion I had to do a repair on an old very tall, highly-polished cabinet TV. The sound circuit had burnt out and I needed to solder a new bias resistor onto the circuit board and replace a valve, PL82, if I remember rightly. I squeezed into the corner of the room behind the large television. The lady had this big black and brown dog, a bulldog type which had two tight testicles that looked as though they had been stuck on just under its stubby tail. This dog had a bad habit of backing up to me with its wagging backside and rubbing its balls on me, and frankly it was getting on my nerves. I said to the woman "You need to call your dog, missis, it's very dangerous for him around here".

"Come here, Basher, you naughty boy" she shouted, then she said "Would you like a cup of tea dear?"

"Yes please" I said. She went to the kitchen and the dog went with her. Relief, I thought, I can get this job done, but then the dog came back with renewed vigour and without its owner he was very bold. I was in the act of soldering when the dog thrust its backside in my face. It startled me and I accidentally touched its balls with my soldering iron. I've never seen anything like it. The dog shot off like a greyhound. It never made a sound, but it hit the back of the settee with such force that it knocked it over backwards. There was an explosion of cushions and newspapers, and a standard lamp crashed onto a coffee table containing a vase of flowers which spilled over, just as the lady was coming out of the kitchen with two cups of tea. I crouched down low behind the television. I didn't have to see what happened, I could hear it "What the dickens?" I heard her say. "You bad boy!" she shouted at him. "I have never seen him behave like that before."

"He was around the back here, I think he must have touched something" I said, biting my lips to fight off laughter. Well, so much for the tea I thought, as she took it back to the kitchen and came out again to clear up. When I went out through the kitchen, I saw the dog sitting on the cold lino floor. As I passed him, he tried to lift one of his bent-over ears but couldn't quite make it, so he rolled his eyes up at me as if to say something like 'all I wanted to do was play ball,' bless him.

I had many wonderful memories, some happy and some sad as I went about repairing televisions in people's houses. The saddest part, of course, was the loneliness some people have, it's heart rending to see it.

Once again it was time to move on. My next job, in 1972, was with a company called the Ditchburn Organisation, and their main office was in Lytham St Anne's, Lancashire. I had a company car and a radio telephone relayed from Grimsby to keep in contact with my local office in Leeds. I took an intensive course at Lytham on automatic phonographs, jukeboxes and other entertainment equipment like fruit machines. The course was in a special part of the factory and during the course I and about four more chaps stayed in a big guest house in Lytham. It's worth a mention, as it was quite an eye opener in some ways. For a start the breakfast looked fantastic at first glance, two thick slices of gammon, two fried eggs, mushrooms, the lot, the only problem was that it wasn't cooked. The fat around the gammon was still semi-transparent and the egg whites were also transparent and I just could not eat it. The only thing that was cooked was the toast, so that and marmalade were all I could eat, and it was like that every morning. I did say something about my breakfast being cooked a bit more, but it was just the same next time.

One of the guys snored. I know everybody snores at some time, but this was something you had to hear to believe it. At eleven o'clock it would start and it reverberated throughout the house. We would knock on his door and he would stop for five minutes, then start again.

But all that was nothing compared to what happened in the early evening when the landlord came back from the pub as we were in the lounge watching TV. He was a smallish guy and quite skinny, and I think he might have been foreign, as he had a slight accent. He came in the room, obviously with a good drink inside him, made a grand bowing gesture, dropped his trousers and underpants and just paraded around the room. One guy said to him "If I had something like that, I wouldn't be bragging about it." He did it every night and we just ignored him. His wife would come in and march him out. If you met him in the morning, he was so very humble and unassuming, he would not look you in the eye and you would think butter wouldn't melt in his mouth.

I gained a company diploma for electromechanical engineering. My working area was vast and stretched from Birmingham to Leeds and the east coast up to Hull, so I spent most of my time travelling from one town to another, visiting pubs at night when everyone was pissed, the jukebox had broken down and I was expected to repair it amongst all the noise, with slopped beer down my neck. It was not fun, especially when I didn't drink, as I didn't in those days. When I got it working again the pub would erupt with cheers and applause then there would be a flood of "Ar mate, I've just put two bob in that fucking thing."

"I'm sorry mate, I can't refund your money but I can give you a free play," I would say.

I soon got to know all the tricks. One of the cheekiest was to push a handkerchief up the returned cash chute so it was out of sight. The customer would press the return button and not receive any money and after making a complaint, the landlord would just give him or her the money back. After a certain period of time the perpetrator would remove the hanky and take all the rejected money. One of the more enterprising antics I saw was when I was called out to a fruit machine in a pub; the landlord had noticed sawdust on the floor around it. At the back someone had drilled a three-inch hole big enough to get a hand in. They must have been very careful, as moving these machines too suddenly would operate an alarm system via a mercury rocker switch. Fortunately they never got any money as it went into a separate metal compartment.

I can't remember exactly how long I worked for this company but one day I got a letter informing me that a firm called the Gains Mead Group was taking over the company and I should carry on working as normal as an engineer until further notice. Eventually I was called to an office in Long Eaton where I met my new manager, and he told me they had different types of machines and to familiarise myself I should attend a training course at a place called Botley, Southampton. This I did and so obtained another diploma. When I returned, I learnt that all the old Ditchburn engineers had been sacked – cutting back on staff, they called it.

A week or so later I was told to report to the office. It was a Monday morning and the manager told me he was sorry but he had to let me go and Friday would be my last day with the company. To be honest it was almost a relief, as I knew it was coming but just didn't know when, and

I wasn't bothered in the least as there were lots of jobs in those days.

I was working in a pub in Grimsby when I got a phone call from the manager, saying he had something very urgent to tell me that he didn't want to broadcast over the radio, and would I please call the office by phone as soon as possible. No rush, I thought to myself, I've still got jobs to do in Grimsby and I didn't want to go back there tomorrow. I knew whatever the manager wanted to say must be important as every pub I visited the landlord said, "Your office rang, would you get back to them." "Oh that's OK, I've spoken to them," I would say, telling a little lie.

It was about six thirty when I arrived at the office and the manager was still there. That's strange, I thought, he usually goes at five. "Ah there you are Dave," he said, "Come in and sit down, had a busy day, have you?" I must admit I had never seen him behave like this. He told me the head office had contacted him that morning and said they had all these Wurlitzer jukeboxes inherited from The Ditchburn Organisation, but we had sacked all the Wurlitzer engineers. He was struggling a little. He left the room and returned with two cups of hot chocolate from the vending machine. "I'll come straight to the point, Dave, I know I gave you your cards this morning, so what I'm saying is, will you please stay on, as you're the only Wurlitzer trained engineer in the company?"

"Well I've never been sacked and reinstated all in one day, so yes," I said.

"You will be getting a rise, of course," he said, pretending to look at some papers. Out of the office I thought to myself, yes mate, and I'm already looking for another job. This company did not have the same camaraderie and friendly attitude as the previous company. It was sad to see all my mates leave one by one, so I thought I was doing my bit for them.

My next job, in 1974, was with a firm called Westrex, an American film company which used to be Western Electric. They changed their name during a period of anti-American feeling in Britain, so I was told. They were responsible for putting film projectors and massive sound systems in just about every cinema in Britain during the big push in cinemas. My office was almost in the centre of Nottingham City centre, underneath the Odeon cinema. My job, apart from emergency breakdown cover of the projectors and sound systems, was to visit all the cinemas that used our equipment and carry out planned preventive maintenance. This was carried out on a monthly basis and was a successful way of keeping things ticking over smoothly, and it also cut down on call outs.

Some of the old cinemas had spectacular equipment installed. The speakers were the size of a small garden shed, and the tweeters that reproduce the high frequencies were at least eight feet long and shaped like a massive old-fashioned gramophone horn, as in the logo of His Master's Voice. This kind of sound engineering gave the big old cinemas that real heart-throbbing ambience, the kind we all remember as kids. The old Westrex engineers, when designing the gradient for the seating, used a ship's sextant to get the precise angle so everyone could see the screen. The powerhouse was a gigantic glass ark mercury rectifier, and sparks like miniature lightning strikes would come out of about a gallon or so of mercury slopping about when it was in operation, and you could smell the ozone gas coming from it. For safety it was housed in a metal cage out of the way, usually in a locked outbuilding. The nearest description I can come up with for this masterpiece is the central control mechanism of the Tardis in the modern Dr Who series.

My time working for Westrex was a happy one, but when the secretary at the city centre office was made redundant, the writing was on the wall. Soon after she had gone the office was closed and used only as a storeroom for spare parts. This was the time when large cinemas were being divided up into smaller ones, making them multi-screen cinemas.

Chapter 9

Open University

~~~~~~

During my employment with Westrex I had a lot of time on my hands as call outs were far less frequent, and I was able to expand my interests. Not having had a formal education I thought it was time to do something about it, so I signed up for a course at the Open University. It was their S100 science course, quite involved and covering just about everything from mathematical formulae to radioactive isotopes and calculating their half-lives. It was what I had always been interested in. Most of the work was done by post, but every now and then I had to meet a real tutor who talked me through certain aspects of the course and assessed how I was getting on.

The time came when I had to go to a real university, and I had the choice of two, Stirling in Scotland or Reading in England. I applied for Stirling but they were full, so Reading it was. It was a week's summer school, as they called it, and for me a bit of a disaster right from the start. I was shown to my room and given a key. On the first night there was a party in one of the halls and so I went. There was dancing and drinking, so not wanting to be left out I joined in, met some of the older students and we had a great time.

When I finally got to my room, I discovered I'd lost my door key. The porter at the main desk said he couldn't do anything until the morning, so I went back to the laundry and tea-making room which happened to be opposite my room and decided I would sleep on the clean laundry shelf. I removed all the towels and such and settled down on the shelf no more than eighteen inches wide. I had driven down by car, so I was quite knackered.

Suddenly the door burst open and four guys poured in, the guys I had met at the gig. They were pissed and very loud. I told them what had happened and they seemed to think their keys might fit, so they all gathered around my door trying their keys. A couple of doors down, a girl opened her door, looked at what was going on and shot back in again. None of their keys fitted, so I got back on my shelf, said thank you and good night lads.

At breakfast I heard a girl saying to some friends of hers, "Last night there were four men trying to break into this poor girl's room". I had a little laugh and said "that poor girl was me" and told them what had happened. I think I pre-empted her tale of woe.

In the science lab the test was to ascertain Le Chatelier's principles of equilibrium, write down what I knew about them and enter the result into the computer. I began entering my results when suddenly the computer started going bonkers and was making a very loud clicking sound. Computers in those days were big, unruly machines and they were most unforgiving of even the slightest spelling mistake which would set them off into meltdown. On the third attempt everybody was standing up from their desks looking at me wondering what the hell I was doing. I raised my hands up in a gesture of defeat and frustration, then sat down.

I seemed to do better in the biology class, although it was not really my subject; I carried on through the week the best way I could and progressed enormously. In the lecture hall I sat near the middle, as it was better for my hearing. During a lecture on tectonic plates and the role they play in continental drift, suddenly everyone turned to face me, the lecturer stopped talking and was also looking at me. Oh bugger, had I farted or something? I turned to the guy next to me and said. "What?"

"Your watch alarm is going off!" he said, nodding to my watch. Oh shit, I must have been the only person in the amphitheatre who couldn't hear it. You must bear in mind I was probably the oldest person in the hall as well, including the lecturer. It seemed to take forever to find the right button to switch it off.

Getting back to my job, travelling about such a lot I met other people doing their own OU courses. Most of them were unemployed, so they had much more time to spend. I think the Open University is the best thing since sliced bread for helping people to get a purpose in life. Being on call twenty-four seven certainly impeded my progress at fulfilling my study schedule and experiments which I had to do, so sadly I had to step down as I was getting too far behind completing my course work.

HMT *Dilwara*

Malayan pygmies

Dave with a viper in the Malayan jungle

Blowing up a giant redwood tree to create a dropping zone

Dave on board a frigate in the South China Sea

Dave coaching the battalion athletics team

Taking the GHQ men for a run

Snake Temple, Penang (photo by C S Foo)

Some of the insects I collected in the jungle

Dave with Alison and Tingo on board the *Hebridean* on the
River Trent, with the *Lady Rowena* in the background

The *Hebridean*

My daughter Corrine

Launching *Chanterelle*, my scallop dive boat, after renovation

Chanterelle after the sinking, with islanders helping

Rebuilding the *Chanterelle's* engine

The re-launching party for *Chanterelle* with Dave, Rex and Jason Rockley and Rosie

Chanterelle rebuilt and relaunched

Taking our hermit, with helpers, to his island on the aluminium boat

Dave and Annabel, alias Sam n' Ella

Annabel

The building of the log house

Dave and Annabel on Easdale Island

Gertrude Matilda

Chapter 10

Property developer

~~~~~~~

A mate was building a small sailing yacht in an old shed at the side of the River Trent and I had watched his progress over several months. I became more and more interested in boat building myself and would spend some of my time hanging out with him. I remember him complaining bitterly about the fact that anything he bought that had anything to do with boats or the pleasure industry had 25% VAT added, a lot more than ordinary household goods. I was in his shed one lunchtime when a chap in an overall came in and asked if he could borrow a hammer, and my mate said cuttingly "We don't use hammers building boats" and turned away from him. The poor chap looked horrified and walked out with his head bowed, so I ran after him to apologise and tell him my mate was just having a bad day.

I moved on from Westrex as the prediction about the writing being on the wall was correct. I sold my semi-detached house and was looking to buy a small cottage in the country, preferably a rundown place as I had very limited funds. To do this I needed ready cash, as it was virtually impossible to get a mortgage on a derelict building. Then I saw an advert in the *Nottingham Evening Post* for a gardener/handyman with a rent-free cottage which went with the job. Oh, I thought, this could be an opportunity to hang on to the profit from the sale of my house, live rent free and get paid while I look around for a cottage to buy, perfect.

I applied for the job and got it. My family and I moved in and I started work right away. There was another worker who was the head gardener; he was in charge of me and he also had a cottage. I worked in the greenhouse, cleaned windows, cleaned the old Bentley, potted up hundreds of geraniums, in fact I did just about everything around the place.

One day I was cleaning the windows of the estate mansion when the lady of the house came up to the window, tapped on the glass and beckoned me to go to the back door. She was a widow living alone in this very large house on the estate, and occasionally her daughter would come home from boarding school to stay and liven up the place. I followed her to the living room where she showed me this large colour television. "It suddenly stopped working, but the sound is all right" she told me. "There was a flash of colour and that was it." Colour TVs were very expensive in those days and there were not too many engineers that could fix them, as it was a whole new ball game, so I could only repair the most obvious faults. The lady wanted to know if I could take it somewhere to get it fixed. Her husband had brought it up from London a few years ago before he died, and there was no contract anywhere to get it repaired. Looks like an off the back of a lorry job to me, I thought.

"Do you mind if I have a quick look at it?" I said.

"What on earth do *you* know about televisions?" she said in a mocking, sarcastic tone.

"I think I might know what's wrong with it, and you say the sound is all right" I said. "I just need to have a quick look in the back to verify my suspicions."

"I am not allowing you to BLOW yourself up in my living room" she said with an exaggerated movement of her arms.

"But honestly, I do know what I'm doing, all I need is a small screwdriver and I have one at the cottage" I said.

"I find all this very hard to believe" she scoffed. "Go and get it then," she said suddenly looking exasperated, "but I will not be responsible for what happens to you."

I got my screwdriver and quickly removed the back. It was a big heavy thing on castors, so it could easily be moved. I soon saw the problem – there was no line generating voltage. This is a transformer which steps the 240 volt AC to about 28,000 volts. In older mono sets the cause of this sort of fault was usually a rectifier valve failure but in this case, there was a solid-state rectifier called a quadrupler which was at fault and I could see where it had burnt out. I took a note of the set make and model, the component number and told the lady I could go and get the part if that was all right, and surprisingly, she agreed. I knew exactly where to get it (it was quite expensive for something that looked like a small three-inch thin stick) and soon I had the part fitted.

She watched every move I made, and with the TV working again her attitude towards me changed considerably. "Who are you, and whatever are you doing here if you have such skills?" she inquired. I had to tell her what my plans were and how I had worked in the television industry. I expected to be sacked on the spot, but quite the opposite, she said I could stay on as long as necessary and wished me good luck with my pending venture.

The price of property was quite low in the mid-sixties, especially old derelict property, but that was all about to change, as I learned later. A pair of old cottages came on the market and they were going to be sold at an auction in Southwell, Nottinghamshire. Now I had never been to an auction before and didn't know the rules. On the day of the auction I turned up with a mate for a bit of moral support. The auction was organised and conducted by a local estate agent. There was quite a large crowd, far more than I had expected, and I was beginning to feel a bit apprehensive about the whole thing. I was also thinking I didn't stand a chance against this lot. My total pot was £3000 and I thought that was a lot for me, but perhaps not for them because this was quite a posh area and there was a lot of money around this part of Nottinghamshire.

The assembly settled down and silence fell over the hall. The auctioneer took up his position on a bale of straw with a sidekick taking notes, and the proceedings began. When the property that I was interested in came up I was a bag of nerves. Get a grip, you silly twit, I told myself. My mate wasn't much help as he was as bad as me. The bidding soon passed the reserve price of £1800 and was still going up and I had not made a bid yet. It got to £3,500 and my heart sank, I looked at my mate and he hunched up his shoulders and said "That's it then, let's fuck off".

"Hang on" I said and started bidding.

"What yer doing, yer daft bugger?" he said. I couldn't see who was bidding against me, but there were at least three other bidders. In for a penny in for a pound I thought, and the bid got up to £6,000. My mate was crapping himself; you would have thought it was his money I was spending. By now there was only one bidder against me. The auctioneer was saying things like "Come on now, this is a builder buying this, just one more, come on now, any more?" I felt like shouting, "I'm not a builder you stupid bastard!" The hammer finally went down to me at £6,300. He had been hanging on to try and get as much as he could to the point of it being almost embarrassing.

So now I had two cottages in about a quarter of an acre, and all I needed to know was how I was going to pay for it. It was £3,300 above my budget. We went for a pint to reflect on what I had just done. Later I found I only had a very short time to come up with the money or the property would be re-auctioned and I would lose everything and still have to pay the auction expenses. Building societies would not grant me a mortgage, as one of the cottages was uninhabitable and the other one had a sitting tenant in it.

It was during a walk with my dog that I got an idea that just might work. I managed to get hold of the owner of the property (I don't remember how I did so) who happened to be a schoolteacher living in Yorkshire. I introduced myself and told him about my predicament and he sounded very sympathetic. I told him I would pay the £3,000 and the auction fee straight away, and I would pay him £40 a month for every month I owed the £3,300 over budget money, which was a very good deal in those days. He agreed and I sent him the money plus any paperwork he needed.

My brother-in-law, Melvin, who was an amazing architect, showed an interest and he drew me up some fantastic plans, as well as an artist's impression of the finished cottage. With the plans, I approached the building society with cap in hand and a packet of chocolate biscuits. They studied the plans and gave me a mortgage almost on the spot. The schoolteacher got his full payment straight away, I didn't have to pay him a single monthly payment and everyone was happy. I had the property. In just over a month, I was working on the first cottage, the one nearest the road, cleaning it out, when a woman came up to me and offered me fourteen thousand cash for just one cottage. I knew then I couldn't go wrong.

I met my sitting tenant, Jack and his wife. He was a retired gamekeeper, and under new ownership he was afraid he might be told to leave. A council official had been to see him and asked if he wanted a flat in the town, and for some reason it had made him worried. I assured him he was welcome to stay as long as he liked. He then asked if his rent would go up I said, "What is the rent and how is it collected?" He told me it was 78 pence a week and he would bring it down to me. "I don't think I will get very fat on that, so we'll leave it as it is" I said.

After serving a week's notice at the big house, I got a job with a building company as a buyer, which meant I had a small clapped-out lorry to collect building materials from builders' merchants and deliver them to the various building sites. My brother Rex was a foreman for this company and a close friend of the owner and when I wasn't on the road with the lorry, I would help him make shuttering for putting a roof on some massive septic tanks he was working on, the wall being built entirely of engineering bricks. They were 16 foot by 16 foot by 7 foot deep, a real work of art. The worst part came when it was time to remove the shuttering and props holding up something like 14 tons of reinforced concrete. This meant getting inside through a two-foot square manhole with a sledgehammer and knocking the props out. If we had got it wrong, we would both have been squashed. It reminded me of my coal mining days. In the winter months starting the lorry in the morning was quite a feat. I literally had to make a fire with oil rags in the air intake, so when the engine was cranked it would suck hot flames into the cylinders and usually start.

Working for this building company I learned a lot; it was a great help getting to know the merchants, and I was able to get some things at trade price for myself. I remember a time I arrived early one morning and so did one of the joiners, and we were waiting for the rest of the workers to turn up. It was a beautiful, sunny morning, so we waited outside. Suddenly falling out of the sky came a queen bumblebee who was being mated by a drone bee. This is something you never see, as it usually happens high in the sky and is very private. "Wow, look at that" I shouted. This guy stepped forward and put his foot down on them hard and said "Arrr, bastard things." I could have hit him. I tried to tell him how special this was, but I knew I was wasting my time. This is a guy who was a professional swearer and he would break up words to get more swear words in. For instance, I would say "What have you got on your sandwiches, Wol?"

"I've got ham and fucking marga-bastard-rine" he would say.

The renovation of my cottage was getting on quite fast and I worked on it whenever I could, day and night. Jack would bring his 78p down the path along with a cup of tea, and say "There's a pantile (terracotta roof tile) missing off my roof and water drips from the ceiling when it rains." I went up the hill with him to have a look. The pan had slid down the roof and was resting in the gutter, and there was no underfelt under the pantiles on roofs in those days. The problem with these old tiles is that the tag that holds them on the batons wears away after a considerable time and the tile slips off. If I had paid a roofer to fix it, I would have been out of pocket rent wise for about three years, so I fixed it myself.

Sadly, old Jack went into hospital and there he died. I don't know what he died from as he seemed quite fit to me and would brag that even in his seventies, he could bend down and touch his toes. His wife said she could not stay there on her own, as it would not be the same without Jack. She left the little cottage and went to live with her daughter. Strangely enough the place wasn't quite the same without my friends up the hill.

My next-door neighbour, Don, in this very small ribbon development village of Upton, was a veterinary surgeon, quite an important one at that, and had his own practice in the next village. At the weekends I would, on occasion, accompany him on his emergency call outs. Once we attended a cow on a remote farm that had suffered a prolapse of the uterus; its womb had slipped out from its normal position along with some major veins and arteries. It was not for the squeamish and even the farmer couldn't bring himself to look. It was the job of the vet to physically push all the contents back into the cow. It was very heavy, sloppy, difficult to handle and there was only a fifty-fifty chance it would all go back in the correct order. Once it was back the opening had to be sewn up, and if any of the veins or arteries ware trapped or kinked the cow would die within a short period of time.

At the other extreme, I attended a call out with him from two elderly ladies who complained their budgerigar was poorly. I followed him into the cottage, and the bird was almost hanging from its perch and looking very sad. Don removed the bird from its cage and said, "Oh I know what's wrong with this little darling, she's egg bound". There was a large intake of breath from both the ladies. "Really?"

"Yes. All we need to do is gently squeeze her and break the shell and that should do it," he said. He had big hands. All we could see was the tip of a beak and he must have squeezed a little too hard because the bird died. What amazed me was, he momentarily tried to put it back on its perch.

I finally finished the work on the cottage and we moved in. It looked exactly like my brother-in-law's artist's representation. One of the first things I did was to make a drive into the property so I had somewhere to park, and I later extended it up the hill to the other cottage, so I had vehicular access to both properties.

Chapter 11

Digging up the past and re-inventing the future

~~~~

My daughter Corrine and I became very interested in collecting old antique bottles, and we spent a lot of time together looking for likely old Victorian rubbish dumps, usually on the outskirts of villages. We found some in Derbyshire and in Yorkshire. It was great fun and we both have wonderful collections. It was quite competitive and we would spend hours digging in likely places where we thought old pots and bottles might have been discarded. I remember digging in an old dump near Southwell racecourse, and in a few minutes I found a beautiful cut-glass perfume bottle top, emerald green and in perfect condition. I said to Corrine "This isn't much good without its bottle", so I threw it away. Shortly after I found the bottle, which was also in fantastic condition. It took all day to re-find the stopper I had thrown away; I still have it to this day.

My interest in boats continued to grow and I got to the stage where I had to have one. I started off with a 26-foot trimaran yacht, quite large for a first boat, which had folding outriggers and was on a road trailer. The boat and trailer I purchased second hand from Llanelli in Wales, and Rex and I drove all the way there to pick it up in my old short-wheelbase Land Rover. What a nightmare that was. It was a nice friendly place with a pub on just about every street corner. As it was a Saturday night and Wales was celebrating winning a rugby match, everyone was in a jovial mood, so we decided to have a half pint of beer in each one. One pub even had its own brewery in the back yard, unheard of in those days.

We only managed to get through about a quarter of the pubs when we met a guy who was interested in what we were doing there and we had a long chat with him. When the pub shouted time, he invited us back to his house for a drink and at about midnight he asked if we wanted anything to eat, so we said that would be very nice. His wife started preparing food and in what seemed like no time at all she came out of the kitchen with a full-blown Sunday dinner, roast beef and potatoes, the lot. It was about two o'clock in the morning when we said we had to go, but the guy insisted we kip down on his sofa and chair. "It's better than your Land Rover," he said, and we agreed.

After a cracking breakfast, we set off to pick up the boat. It was enormous, twenty-six feet long and made the Land Rover look tiny. Rex immediately said "It's too big to be towed by this" and patted the bonnet of the Rover. Well I must confess it did look that way. The boat was in the bloke's back yard, and how he got it in there I can't imagine, all I do know is that it took most of the morning to get it out. The chap didn't show up till it was on the road ready to go.

There was a bridge across the narrow road, which we had not considered. "It's not going to go under that" I said, but it did, with about an inch to spare. I had been down there the week before, when I had sailed the boat, bought and paid for it.

The journey back to Nottingham was pure hell. If we went above thirty-five miles per hour the boat would start snaking from side to side and lifting the back end of the Land Rover, and there was nothing we could do to prevent it other than slow down. Getting home seemed to take forever.

I sailed this boat for three or four years on the River Trent, which was where I did a lot of sail training. It's surprising how difficult it is sailing on a fast-flowing river. There was an embarrassing occasion when I was sailing down the river travelling at the same speed as the river was flowing. I wanted to alter course so I put the tiller over, but nothing happened and I crashed into the bank. At first I thought the rudder had fallen off. There were people watching on the riverbank, so I jumped off with a rope as if it had been intentional.

I learned a lot in those early days and because of the size of the boat it was so much harder. I remember one time I was moored alongside the bank having a cup of tea when an old guy in a small sailing dinghy came to within a couple of feet of my boat. He was still sailing whilst he was talking to me and had perfectly matched the strength of the wind with the flow of the river, and he was doing it without looking, his hands were constantly adjusting the main sheet and jib while all the time he was asking me questions about my boat. I said to myself, when I can do that with a yacht this size or bigger, I will be able to call myself a yachtsman. I never forgot it, and I can honestly say I did achieve that skill after a few years. I went on to sail this boat in the North Sea and off the coast of Wells Next the Sea. I also trailed it up to Argyll in Scotland, and there I got to know certain parts of the Scottish west coast and fell in love with its wildness.

My next boat was a 37-foot snow goose catamaran. Being unable to afford a completed boat I settled for just the empty hull with the one main bulkhead fitted for rigidity in transport. It was delivered to a field belonging to a friend of mine in Nottinghamshire by police escort all the way from Canvey Island. I had sailed the same sized yacht in the Thames estuary off the coast at Southend on Sea and was very impressed by it. The driver of the delivery lorry was a thalidomide victim. Thalidomide was a synthetic drug used as a sedative and given to pregnant woman to help with morning sickness but found to cause severe abnormalities in the developing foetus. He only had small stumps for his arms and legs, but he really was quite amazing. The lorry had been specially fitted out so he could reach all the controls, and there was even a system fitted for lifting him in and out of the cab. At the sight of all this, I suddenly realised my mouth was wide open and I had to swallow the lump in my throat.

This boat on dry land was massive and the amount of work needed to finish it was somewhat overwhelming. The inner space was so big it had an echo in it, and I began to wonder if I had bitten off more than I could chew. My original plan was to fit out the boat and sail it to the Greek islands in the Aegean Sea where I would charter it to make a living. But I had spent a lot of time sailing in Scotland and I had fallen in love with the place, so a change of plan was on the cards. By now my wife and I had split up and we shared the property, a cottage each. I sold mine to finance my chosen path in life.

When I really got into fitting out the yacht and could see how I was getting on, I set myself a deadline for getting the boat finished. I set up a yacht chartering business and registered for VAT. I then started advertising in the magazines and local newspapers and got quite a few interested replies.

Using glass fibre resin inside a closed cabin area was not a good idea and I remember spending so long in the confined space breathing in the fumes that when I finally went outside into the cockpit, I was so dizzy I fell off the boat. It was a good eight or nine feet from the ground, and my shoulder missed a large jack plane on the ground by a fraction of an inch. If I had hit the tool it would have been game over. I suffered a lot of pain in my shoulder and neck because of the fall, which affected my work output. After that I would do a little at a time with plenty of fresh air blowing through the boat. Fitting the engine and aligning it up with the prop shaft was quite a challenge, but I got there, eventually.

When the boat was ready for launching into the River Trent it cost more to move it the four miles to the river than it had cost all the way from Canvey Island to Nottinghamshire. To do this I was told to buy, at great cost, an RSJ (steel H girder), which was needed to help lift the boat into the river, and of course useless to me after, so the boatyard ended up having it.

With the boat now on the river I could test the engine and carry on fitting her out. The local radio station heard about me and what I intended to do, so they came and interviewed me, and next morning I was on the radio. A couple of days later a TV crew turned up and I gave them a sail on the river while they interviewed me, so for five minutes I was a TV star. I had sold my property, so from now on the boat was my home and my work place. I still had quite a lot of fitting out to do, which I would do on passage, I hoped.

The day finally arrived when I was to set sail for the west

coast of Scotland; it was April 1984. I somehow knew this was to be a life-changing adventure. My crew consisted of Trevor, Alison the chef and my oldest brother, Fred. We boarded the boat at Gunthorpe on the River Trent and set off. It was a fairly straightforward journey down the river, but by the time we got to where the river becomes tidal, after Cromwell Lock, we were all very tired. Now we were in brackish water and navigating a narrow stream in the middle of sloping banks of glutinous mud both sides, and it was getting difficult to keep the boat from going aground, which it did several times. We made it as far as Keadby, where we tied up against a small jetty for the night. We did venture to the local pub which was a short walk away. The locals were very surprised to see us at that time of night and in April. We told them what we were doing and got lots of advice, along with some tales of woe, like being stuck in the mud for days until the tide was big enough to lift the boat again.

Next day we were pushing a very strong tide and we met the Aegir, a tidal bore. It was not a big one, but it was high enough to lift the boat and bang us onto the river bed. Sailing into the Humber we needed to look for diesel fuel, so we headed for Immingham Docks, probably the largest refinery in the country. Of course we couldn't get anywhere near it for the massive tankers moored there, so we approached and came alongside a large tug type of boat. It was much higher than we were and I shouted to a man aboard her "Hello there! Do you know where we could get some diesel from?"

He came to the side of the tug and looked down on us. He stood with hands on hips and scanned the boat from stem to stern. His boiler suit glistened with the amount of grease on it and it was hard to imagine its original colour.

"HOW MUCH DO YOU WANT?" he growled very loudly.

"Two jerry cans full would do it" I replied. I could have done with more but didn't want to seem greedy or a nuisance. He disappeared for a minute or two, came back and shouted. "TIE YOUR CANS TO THIS ROPE". Then he threw a very thick, oily yellow rope down. It was too thick to go through the jerry can handles, so I tied a thinner rope to the thick one and he pulled up the cans. I was now a bit worried he might not fix the full and heavy cans well enough and I had visions of them smashing through the deck.

In less than five minutes his face appeared over the gunwale and he shouted "STAND YER BY!" I have no idea where he got the diesel from or how he got it into the cans, but he lowered the cans down one at a time, and I was somewhat relieved.

"How much do I owe you?" I shouted up.

"ARR BE 'WAY WI YA, I SPILL MORE'N THAT IN A BLOODY DAY!" he said in a boasting sort of manner, but still growling.

"Thank you very much" I said, but he had gone. What a kind growling man, I thought, it just goes to show you. "A simple act of kindness" I said.

We now headed across the Humber for Spurn Head, where we could rest and plan how to step the forty-foot anodised aluminium mast which had lain across the deck for so long. As we passed the lifeguard lookout station at Spurn Point they gave us a blast on their fog horn as a warning. We were heading towards a submerged shipwreck, but I had already spotted it on my chart, so we were giving it a wide berth. We sailed on past it to an anchorage a good distance from the wreck and well out of any eddying currents.

Next day was a perfect day for raising the mast, no wind and very calm conditions. We laid out all the rigging with halyards attached, forestays and backstays all fitted. The mast went up no problem at all, but before we could get the stays fixed and tightened the boat began to pitch and roll. There was a violent swell and with an uncontrolled, very heavy mast waving about, the deck suddenly became a very dangerous place to be. Because of the hinged foot of the mast it could only fall one way – backwards. I shouted to the crew who were struggling in vain to hold on to it as the swell got worse. "Let it go!" It fell off the aft of the boat with half of it in the sea, and the mast shoe was ripped off. The anemometer, wind direction indicator and radio antenna were all destroyed. The reason for this sudden unforeseen swell was that unknown to us a massive tanker had sailed out of the Humber, and we got the swell from it about twenty minutes later.

It's difficult to put into words just how I felt at that time. I was tempted to abort the mission and go home, but then

I remembered I hadn't got a home to go back to, and I had paying customers who had booked and paid in advance. The crew understood, and they left me alone for a while until they felt it was all right to bring me a cup of tea.

With all my tools on board, Trevor and I soon figured out how to fix the mast foot, and we were ready for another attempt at stepping the mast. There was nothing I could do about the masthead equipment – I would just have to replace it all when I was able to buy it, climb the mast and fit it. We decided not to step the mast there but wait for somewhere more settled, perhaps not even try to step it again until we were aground.

Out into the North Sea we went to continue our journey north. Unfortunately, it was by engine, as the damage to the mast and rigging was worse than I thought. As I motored out of the Humber and into the North Sea I said to the crew "This is our last chance, if I turn right, we go to the Aegean Sea, if I turn left it's Scotland." I was only joking of course but everyone yelled "LEFT!"

Chapter 12

A life on the ocean wave

Our first port of call was Bridlington. It was just getting dark when we arrived, and we were encouraged on by a fantastic smell of fish and chips wafting out to sea. No sooner had we moored in the harbour against the wall when a gentleman from the Royal Yorkshire Yacht Club came up and introduced himself, and invited us to the yacht club, saying we could have access to the club's facilities. I gladly accepted. It was a very friendly atmosphere in the yacht club, where I signed their club logbook and we got to chat with the club members over a pint or two. We told them we were hoping to step the mast tomorrow at low water and they offered their help should we need it.

Next day the tide was out, so the boat was dried out on hard sand. We erected the mast with no problems, fitted all the rigging and now the boat was ready for her sea trials under sail. We said goodbye to Trevor, who unfortunately had to go home, but not before he gave Fred and me a haircut in the open cockpit. It attracted quite a crowd, I don't know why, and there was some friendly banter from the folk looking on.

The rest of the day was taken up tidying the boat, getting the sails fitted with their roller reefing and so on. Next day we said goodbye to the yacht club members, who came down to see us off. With a man short getting out of the harbour was very tricky. Turning a thirty-seven foot by fifteen-foot beam boat within its own length in a tightly-packed space was not going to be easy. Lucky for me a bystander seemed to want to take charge and he knew a thing or two. He borrowed a large orange buoy from a fishing boat, which he used as a fender, and managed to turn the boat within its own length, and he never even came aboard. I must confess I was impressed.

We were bound for Beacon Hill off Flamborough Head, and with the sails up we made steady progress, but very soon the wind died and we were back on engine. I could see there was more work to do with the rigging, but for now our main task was getting to the west coast.

And so on to Scarborough. We arrived at 2210 hours and settled in East Harbour. There must have been fog at sea, because in the early hours of the morning the foghorn went off and I hovered above my bunk for a second or two. Every minute there was a five-second blast of the fog signal and it seemed like we were right underneath it. Not a lot of sleep was had for the rest of that night and to add salt to our wounds I had to pay harbour dues of £7.98 for twenty-four hours – that was expensive in those days. So we didn't hang around in Scarborough.

Next stop on our journey was a long one – we were going all the way to Blyth harbour – so that meant an early start. On arrival at 1915 hours we were allocated a berth in the south harbour and were greeted by the Royal Northumberland Yacht Club. They too made us very welcome and offered us all their amenities. The yacht club's headquarters were in a houseboat called Tyne. There wasn't a lot to do so we had an early night, as we were quite shattered after a long day. Again, a very early start and a long passage to the Farne Islands, which we passed on passage to the Holy Island. We anchored in the bay and went ashore to visit the village and have a look around. We also sampled the sweet mead which they make on the island, and it was very good. Although this was not a good place to spend the night, the weather forecast was good, so we stayed.

Next port of call was Stonehaven in Scotland, quite an easy harbour to enter, and because this time of year the harbour was not busy, the harbour master gave us the necessary permission to stay and we spent the night against the harbour wall. The harbour dues were twenty pence a foot. We were able to get whatever provisions we needed, so the next port was Peterhead, which was a long haul as it had become very foggy.

As we approached the entrance to the harbour, which we could just make out through the thick fog, the engine cut out and we were drifting towards some rocks just outside the entrance. It could not have happened at a worse time. I radioed the harbour master to see if he could be of assistance. We got no help from him at all. I hastily got into the engine compartment to have a quick look at what the fault might be and discovered a diesel leak on the main fuel supply pipe. I managed to repair it with a couple of jubilee clips and a short length of 10mm plastic pipe. I quickly tried to start the engine, which started after a few agonising attempts, thank goodness – it had a self-bleeding fuel system fitted. An oil rig support vessel was moored just inside the harbour and he radioed that he could see us on his radar and we should follow his directions for getting into the harbour. Once safely in the harbour bay, I thanked the skipper of the support vessel for all his help.

The fog by now was a real pea-souper and it stayed like that for a solid week – we began to wonder if it would ever lift. When the fog finally did start to thin, we got a visit from the coastguard telling us there was a storm coming in and that it would be safer if we moved into the inner harbour. As it was, we were anchored in the bay and not a good place to be in bad weather as we would be on a lee shore.

Getting into the inner harbour was like going through a maze. It seemed to go on and on, and even a bridge had to be raised to allow for the mast. We got to the far end and tied up against the wall, to find that there was a ladder set into the wall but it was dripping in thick black oil. The fenders were also covered in the stuff – because this was a backwater the oil never got washed away and so it accumulated.

Then out of the blue two Customs and Excise officers in full uniform wanted to come aboard down the oily ladder, wearing blue disposable gloves as they didn't want to get their hands oily. They wanted to inspect the log book and ask some questions. The younger one said to me "What was your last port of call, sir?" And you know what, I could not remember, my brain had gone a complete blank. The older guy had an understanding smile, as if to say "Yah, I have them too." Then the chef, Alison, intervened and said, "It was Stonehaven."

"Yes, that's the place" I said, "the harbour dues were £7.40p."

"Thank you, sir, that's all we want to know. Good day to you," and off they went. They never looked at the logbook. Now all we had to do was get the oil from their shoes off the deck.

That evening we went ashore to explore the docks, and found that the bad weather had brought fishing boats in to shelter, dozens of them. Some poor souls must still have been out there, as the lifeboat was launched – it was quite impressive seeing it go down the steep ramp and making a tremendous splash. Well one good thing, the gales had shifted the fog, so now it was time to think about getting out of this oil bath, which wasn't going to be easy as there was not enough room to manoeuvre. We had noticed a small tugboat nipping about here, there and everywhere and what this guy couldn't do with his boat wasn't worth thinking about, watching him handle his tug was quite amazing. When he was close to our boat, I asked him if he could pull our bow out. He was a friendly chap and in no time at all he had us out of a very tight corner which we had been shunted into by the fishing boats. As soon as he had our bow out from the wall we were off and anchored again in the bay where we had come from. We spotted something quite large drifting toward us, and couldn't make it out at first but as it got closer, we realised it was a huge grey seal without a head, probably decapitated by a ship's prop or something.

Those extra ten days added to our journey, which forced a change of circumstances and the two-remaining crew had to leave for their own personal reasons. I rowed them ashore in my dinghy and we said our goodbyes. Alison the chef was to come back and re-join the boat at a later date, depending on where I was. That gave me the opportunity to work on finishing some jobs on the boat.

Next day I weighed anchor and set off. I was now single-handed and to be honest feeling quite lonely. The visibility was good, so I could continue my journey north. About three miles off Rattray Head I was visited by a pod of huge grey bottle nose dolphins, there were five or six but it was difficult to know just how many. They circled the yacht with ease, seemingly without any effort, and I was doing twelve knots. The largest one raised itself out of the sea on its tail and looked at me in the cockpit, nodding its head slightly, then they all took it in turns to do the same, some two at a time. I got a length of spare roller reefing pipe, stuck it in the sea off the stern and shouted down it to try and communicate with them, but to no avail. Their behaviour lasted about ten minutes in all, then at some unheard signal they shot off at a forty-five-degree angle to my course, all at once, and were soon out of sight. I felt suddenly very sad and shed an emotional tear. To be alone with these majestic creatures in their own environment was overwhelming to say the least, I only wish I could have spoken to them, asked them questions, anything to keep them with me.

In all this excitement I had gone way off course. I soon corrected it and was now heading for Fraserburgh with the inevitable smell of fish and chips wafting offshore. Instead of trying to get into the harbour I anchored in the bay just offshore. It was about lunch time and I was still excited about the dolphins, so I decided to go ashore for a pint. The nearest pub overlooking the bay seemed all right, so in I went. I stood at the bar and a chap about my age asked where I had come from as he could see I wasn't local. "It's a long story," I told him, and said I was anchored in the bay. "Uh oh, it's not safe to stay there" he said, having looked at the yacht through the window.

"Well I don't intend to stay that long," I told him

"Look, the harbour master is a personal friend of mine, I'll take you to meet him and see if there's a berth, it won't cost you anything, and I can help you bring the boat in." It seemed a good idea at the time. He introduced me to the harbour master, and he told me exactly where to go, against a wall a good fifteen foot high, but it had a ladder built into the wall so that was OK.

With the yacht safely moored up we set off to get another pint, and the guy said "Why don't we go to the ex-serviceman's club as a pint is half price there?" so we did. I got on very well with some of the older guys and we reminisced about army life and our experiences and the pints kept on coming. We left the club and now, with a few pints in us, we hit the town proper. This guy took me on a tour of the best pubs, but they all seemed the same to me. At one particular pub a woman asked me if I would like to go to a party. I had seen this woman at another pub earlier. Well I'm all for a party, so I said "Where is it?"

"We must get a taxi" she said.

The guy came up to me and I told him about the party.

"Not a good idea" he said, "but if you are going, I'll come with you." There was quite a gang of us in two taxis, and we headed off into a large housing estate. It wasn't one party, there were three in different houses, all close to one another. Well, by now I did not know if I was coming or going. The guy, whose name I cannot remember, got lost somewhere, while I landed up on a settee at this woman's house and she was getting rather amorous. Truth is I couldn't raise an eyebrow, let alone anything else. She got the message and left me alone on the settee.

There were other bodies in the room somewhere as I could hear them snoring. I awoke early and got out straight away. Trouble is I had no idea where the hell I was or where the boat was, so I followed my nose and continued downhill towards the sea. I found the harbour and went to my boat. It had been moved and a fishing boat was in my boat's place, which the harbour master had given me. Well I didn't mind that, what got me was the way they had tied it up. Some pillock had tied the ropes too tight and on a falling tide which had left the boat almost hanging from its cleats, you would not expect that from a fisherman.

I managed to get the boat sorted and got on board, where I spent the day licking my wounds, so to speak. I was awoken from a doze by a loud thump. It was about six o'clock in the evening and the harbour wall was moving past the window, couldn't make it out for a minute. Then I realised the boat was being pulled towards a wall ladder; I went to look out of the aft cabin window in time to see one youth on the boat and two more on the ladder. My survival hackles were up and I burst through the door making as much noise as possible and in my loudest army voice shouted "What the fuck are you doing?"

Well, I have never seen anybody move so fast. The youth on the deck leaped at the ladder, slipped badly and must have hurt himself, as he was hanging momentarily, but he got his footing and was gone. There were four of them in all, and they would most likely have taken the life raft which was strapped to the deck (it was on hire and worth about two grand), or broken into the cabin and helped themselves and who knows what havoc they would have wrought. I stayed vigilant most of the night expecting them to return with perhaps more of them, so I didn't get much sleep.

At first light I was on my way and motored out before the fishermen. After a hard push I got as far as Burghead Bay and was absolutely shattered, having been up most of the night and had a late night the night before it had all caught up with me. Burgead harbour seemed a bit narrow for me to get into single handed so I anchored in the bay.

Just before dusk the wind started to freshen up and the forecast was for onshore winds force five to six, occasionally seven, gale eight later. I did not like the sound of that and knew I had to get shelter somewhere and get off this lee shore. The only other place was Findhorn, which looked like a safe anchorage – the problem was that in the winter months the yacht club take in their marker buoys showing the navigable channel. Before it became too dark, I lined up the boat with the channel and what I thought was the passage, going by the different colours of the sea and sand, which gave me an idea of where the shallows were – the tide was almost out. When I had my bearings, I deliberately went aground to wait for the tide to return and pray the bad weather held off till I was inside the anchorage.

I dropped the anchor to stop the boat drifting away too

far from my position. The tide finally came back, but all tides seem to take forever, especially when you're waiting for them.

The wind was now whistling in the rigging and waves were slapping at the hull. I was getting a bit worried as it was also pitch black and all I had to go on was the compass bearing I had taken earlier.

Suddenly the boat swung round to face the anchor, which meant I was afloat, and the tide was coming back quickly. I had a very powerful lamp with a long beam which I made ready for action. Another hour and I had enough water under me to try for the channel. I weighed anchor, turned the boat and set off; the wind was pushing me towards the shore faster than I really wanted to go. I had to go astern now and again to slow down. Finding the deepest water with my depth sounder, I followed the pre-set compass course which I had taken when I lined up the boat to the harbour channel. I could hear the waves crashing on the shore both sides of me. Inside the channel I picked my way using the torch to avoid all the mooring buoys or whatever they were, and when I was clear of all obstructions, I dropped the anchor, hit my bunk and slept like a baby.

Next morning was Sunday, and after a bit of a lie in I could hear voices, so I looked out of the window to see a crowd of people gathered in front of a building, all looking at me. Oh dear, have I broken some rules or what? A chap in a rowing boat came alongside and asked me when had I got in. I said "About two o'clock this morning."

"Nobody comes in here, in winter, specially at night with a boat this size" he replied.

"Who are all those people?" I said "Have I done something wrong?"

"Oh no, most of them are members of the Royal Findhorn Yacht Club and they want to meet you," he said. "If you would like to go over, I'll take you, the bar will be open if you want a pint." This guy must have read my mind, I thought.

"Give me a minute, I've not even cleaned my teeth yet." I got in his boat and said "Hang on, how will I get back aboard?"

"Don't worry about that." Ashore I met some of the club members and they all seemed to be intrigued as to how I had managed to get into the harbour at night and single handed. They were saying things like there were constant shifting sandbanks out there and the marker buoys weren't put out until springtime. Well I did know all about that from the sailing directions and the pilot book I had on the yacht. It's amazing what you can do when you have to.

I was made very welcome at the yacht club and treated almost like royalty; I think of the sixteen days I was there, I only spent two nights on my boat. Some of the members were serving RAF personnel and there was always a dinner or a party to go to in the evening. I met a gentleman who was a retired French attaché; he gave me his card and invited me to his home at Fort William on the west coast, and as I was to eventually sail past Fort William, having come through the Caledonian Canal on passage to the west, I did stop to pay him and his family a visit. I had many a night drinking and eating with the club's Commodore of the day and on one occasion he said I should be made an honorary member of the yacht club and he would look into it. Thirty-three years later I returned to the yacht club to see if I had indeed been made an honorary member. I told my story to one of the senior members of the club and he found my name in the club's log book of that year, 1984, but unfortunately, I hadn't been made a member. The staff suggested that it must have been the drink talking on the commodore's part. Well so much for that, but not to worry, I had a lovely meal and seeing the place again brought back some fond memories.

I was invited one afternoon to the Findhorn Foundation to see what they were all about and I was fascinated. People from all over the world were staying there doing different studies and just enjoying themselves. I was shown the so-called 'giant' vegetables but, coming from an agricultural area, they looked just like ordinary veg to me. I thoroughly enjoyed my visit to the centre and was utterly amazed to see how it had grown when I visited it again thirty-three years later.

Now it was time to move on. I still had a long way to go. One of the guys had said to me one night at the bar, "You know, Dave, if you don't bugger off soon, you'll get port bound and end up staying here just like me."

My crew, Alison, who was also the chef, turned up as

promised, and we had one last drink and meal in the club and said our goodbyes. We were off to Inverness and the Caledonian Canal. Sailing Loch Ness was very exciting, but going through the canal was not a very happy experience at all. Pity about the lock keepers, they seemed a miserable lot for some reason or other – all they had to do was press a button to open and close the gates. With just the two of us on board we were finding it difficult to cope with controlling the boat, and they would not take a rope or help in any way whatsoever. As soon as we were in the lock, they would turn their backs to us, no happy repartee, no hellos, no good mornings, nothing. Maybe it was a union-controlled thing, I don't know, but I can honestly say I was so pleased to get out of there. What was quite amazing was they had a speed limit for going through the canal, but if you didn't make it to the last lock in time you had to pay a fee to get out or spend the night there. I followed a fishing boat all the way through and was able to keep up with him. At one of the last locks, the skipper of the fishing boat couldn't stand it any longer and shouted to me over the noise of the engine, "What the hell have you got in there?"

"I have a thirty horsepower Nanni diesel," I shouted back.

"Never heard of it" he said, and vanished into his wheelhouse. It's an Italian make of engine and it served me very well. As for the passage through the locks, I could quite easily write a whole chapter on the lock keepers' behaviour, but I would rather not. Having said that, there are probably a new set of guys now, new rules, and maybe more friendly too.

From Fort William to Dunstaffnage Bay was an enjoyable sail, as I was now entering familiar waters. Here I had to rest and wait for the tide to slack out, so I could get into Loch Etive. The tide runs out of the loch at over eight knots and at spring tides probably more, and it becomes a sea waterfall, one of the few in the world, so it's very important to get the timing right as it's extremely dangerous if you don't. This is also why very few boats venture up this loch. If you can't go faster than the water is flowing you will not have any control over your vessel. Luckily my boat could cruise under engine at twelve knots and up to twenty plus under sail.

I made my base near the village of Taynuilt in Argyll and that was where I would run my business from. I had first fallen in love with this place when I sailed my trimaran on this loch and spent a month exploring it with my daughter Corrine on board, and we had some wonderful adventures. Of course, it also meant getting out of the loch, which was sometimes a bit of a strain on the old bowels, especially when actually sailing down what can only be described as a waterfall into the Atlantic Ocean and being carried along by very strong currents. When you think about it, there's about fourteen miles of loch pouring into the sea and then you have the whole Atlantic desperately trying to get back in when the tide changes.

Chapter 13

Yacht charter time

～～～

It was getting close to the date for my first paying guests to arrive, so it was panic stations getting everything shipshape. A specific request from one of the guests was for smoked kippers for breakfast at some time. Well I can honestly say you're not going to believe this, I tried everywhere in Oban to get some kippers but to no avail – even Bookers, the wholesale outlet where I had an account, didn't have any. I gave up and headed back to base and just as I was about to turn off the main road at a T-junction, I came across a box in the middle of the road. Some of its contents were scattered around, and I said to Alison, "Blimey, they look like kippers."

"They are kippers!" she yelled. I stopped and gathered them up, and they were in perfect condition, shrink-wrapped and straight off the back of a lorry, Orkney light smoked golden kippers, about twenty packs of them, two kippers per pack. I must say they were delicious. I gave some to my friends and took the rest on board the yacht. Coincidences like this do not happen very often and I was thankful for it. I have told this story to quite a few friends of mine since and I could never tell whether they actually believed me or not, but it is honestly true.

An old mate had travelled up from Nottingham to see how I was getting on with my sailing career. He was the mate who had introduced me to sailing boats in the first place, but he had not sailed on the sea before, just the river Trent. Two other guests I had to pick up from Oban railway station. One was a bank manager who worked in Kuwait, and he loved sailing in Scotland and came over every year, the wetter the better for him he told me. The other guest was a reporter from the *Nottingham Evening Post*, who was to write a feature about her adventure for the paper on her week's sail aboard the yacht *Hebridean*, and it was a nice bit of advertising for me, as it turned out.

On our sail to Oban it was blowing about a force six. When we got out of the loch and into open sea, I could see my mate was looking very pale and alarmed. "There are white horses out there," he pointed out in a panicking sort of tone. Of course, it was nothing to what I had been used to and so I assured him it was perfectly all right, the boat could handle it. A cruise around the Isle of Mull and visiting the small islands of Coll, Tiree, the Treshnish Isles and Staffa is a nice steady week's cruise and I did a lot of them during the season.

Back on my Crown Estate registered mooring at Achnacloich, Loch Etive, I met a guy called Mike Campbell who was working on an old decommissioned fishing boat which he had bought at a giveaway price. It would become his home as well as a working scallop diving boat when he had converted it. There was an old French engine fitted, the type you could add cylinders to or take them away from, could never understand why, and it was a work of art starting that engine. Mike would go down into the engine room clean and come out looking like a different nationality. It had to be started by compressed air from a dive bottle and there was a tremendous amount of black smoke during the starting process issuing from the deck hatch.

One day Mike invited me on board for a drink and to show me a wood-burning stove he had just fitted. He said he had found the flue pipe in an old shed and thought it would do nicely. He had his girlfriend on board and we were sitting around the stove having a blether and he had got the stove red hot, burning a mixture of wood and coal. It was very nice considering how bitterly cold it was outside. He had just opened a bottle of Martini when there was a loud bang, a flash of fire and hot ash and smoke filled the cabin. The flue pipe had disintegrated and the air became very toxic. I was up on deck in seconds and shouted down the hatch "Are you all right down there" his girlfriend appeared looking dusty but all right, and Mike followed her out from below. "What the bloody hell was that?" I enquired

"It was the damn flue pipe, it blew up, must have had some air pockets in it or something."

"But I thought it was asbestos," I said

"So, did I, can't understand it," Mike said.

We got on really well, went on to become great mates and had lots of adventures together, as you will read. That incident reminded him of another occasion when he had worked on an old puffer boat on the Isle of Mull, with the job of lifting sunken coal from a very old shipwreck in the Sound of Mull. They had a hydraulically-operated grab bucket on board the old puffer which they used to lift the coal from the seabed and then would sell it to residents of Mull and small islands such as Easdale, and they also used it to power their steam puffer boat. The skipper of the puffer was a man called Hughie Carmichael, a lovely chap who I met once through Mike. They were in Craignure on the Isle of Mull when a yacht went aground on a falling tide with a family of four on board. The yacht was leaning over at an uncomfortable angle and there was a very strong offshore wind gusting up to gale force, preventing them from rowing ashore. With no engine on their rubber dinghy they would surely have been blown into the sound of Mull and beyond, had they tried.

Hughie saw the predicament they were in and set about

a rescue plan. He went into the wheelhouse, where he had a rocket-powered rope thrower, the kind used by the coastguard to get a line onto a stricken vessel. This one had seen better days; it was rusted up from years on board the boat in a salty environment. Mike had told him to get rid of it a few days before, but Hughie liked to hang on to things. He came out and saw the family standing on the gunwales of the boat in perfect graduation formation, dad, mum, son and daughter, then aimed the rocket launcher high to go way over the yacht and fired. Nothing happened. He banged it on the guard rail and tried again, still nothing.

So Hughie took it into the wheelhouse to give it some thought. He attacked it with the only tool he had on board, a hammer; according to Hughie everything could be fixed with a hammer. It was the trigger mechanism that was at fault, so he gave it a damn good hammering. The rocket went off in the wheelhouse with a huge explosion that rocked the boat. The rocket was flying around in the confined space of the wheelhouse, spewing rope over everything. The thick white smoke made it impossible to see anything, the rope snagged on the wheel and this made the rocket go around in circles like a Catherine wheel.

Mike heard the racket and ran on deck to see what was going on – he could hear Hughie but not see him. Now Hughie was a man who never swore – his equivalent to the F-word, was 'by crikey'. That was all Mike could hear coming out of the wheelhouse, but he knew what had happened. Hughie suddenly burst out of the wheelhouse in a vortex of swirling smoke, draped in string from the rocket, coughing and spluttering and holding his wrist as if he was keeping his jet-black burnt hand from falling off.

"By crikey Mikey, I never expected that," he said.

Mike replied, "What the bloody hell do you expect, hitting it with that bloody hammer of yours?"

They both turned like clockwork figures to hear a faint "Hello!" coming from the yacht. The family were still in perfect position, the dad waving his hand from shoulder height as if not wanting to make too much fuss but to remind them they were still waiting to be rescued. Hughie said "By crikey I'd forgotten about them, what can we do?"

Mike said, "Doing what you should have done in the first place, letting the wind blow a buoy down to them with a rope attached. They can tie it to their dinghy and we can pull them ashore". When the family came ashore, they had been watching with interest, thinking the explosion was all part of the rescue plan.

As a result of the article in the *Nottingham Evening Post* written by the reporter who had been for a cruise on my yacht, three guys booked for a week's cruise. The first night was spent at anchor in Tobermory Bay on the Isle of Mull. We were all having a drink in the Mishnish Inn when I met an old friend of mine, Markie Dan. He was the skipper of a scallop dredger, and his boat was moored alongside the harbour wall. Markie was an amazing poet – he could make up a poem instantly about any subject you could wish for and recite it fluently. After closing time, he invited us on board for a dram and to show off his new GRP plotter, the size of a small TV, which kept a record of all his dredging runs so he didn't go over the same ground twice.

When we were about to leave, Markie told us to take some of the fish he had caught as a by-catch in his dredging gear. They looked somewhat tattered and bruised but were otherwise all right, so I took what I needed and went back to the yacht. Sadly, Markie is no longer with us, but I wonder what he would say if he knew a pub in Oban had been named after him.

Next day it was blowing near gale force winds in the bay, so it would have been much worse in the open sea. I said to the lads "Are you sure you want to do this?" and they said "Yerr, let's go for it". We set off and I got them gutting and filleting the fish on the aft deck. We sailed into the sound of Mull and were soon approaching the notorious Ardnamurchan Point, which we had to sail around to visit the Small Isles; Eigg, Rum, Muck, and Canna. The sea was getting really rough, because even in calm conditions it can still be rough in this area due to conflicting tidal streams.

I told the lads to get into the cockpit for safety and leave the fish there. They had become very quiet and by now were looking yellowish grey in colour, and they seemed to have lost that all important adventure attitude. As I rounded the point, they were hanging over the rails and throwing up, looking very desperate. I started the engine and reefed the sails, as I had to get them ashore somewhere as soon as possible, I didn't want to ruin their holiday.

There was an entrance a short distance from Ardnamurchan Point to a small bay, not really defined on the Admiralty chart, so I motored in. It was bigger than it first appeared and there was a little cottage hidden away in a sheltered position with fishing nets draped across tall wooden frames to dry. I anchored and rowed the guys ashore. They were so happy to be on solid ground and after a good walk they recovered surprisingly well.

With the guys back on board I was in the act of weighing anchor when I noticed a man in a small boat with a young girl sitting in the bow. He was rowing as fast as he could, his arms going like a fiddler's elbow playing *Flight of the Bumble Bee*. It was the man from the cottage. When he got close, he shouted "Why didn't you visit me, I would have given you a salmon!"

We were lost for words momentarily, but then we had a little chat with him. He told us that no one ever comes into his wee bay, it was so isolated where he lived. Then he said, "Do you have any tea you could let me have?" Alison gave him a handful of tea bags and one of the guys gave the little girl a Mars bar, which she accepted with wide open eyes and a big smile. After apologising for not visiting him and promising I would in a future similar situation, we all went on our journey, happy and smiling. I had to laugh when one of the guys called the safety rail around the gunwale of the boat a balustrade, but being an architect and landlubber, he was forgiven.

On one of the small islands we visited we were watching the coming and going of cormorants and shags. The shags were nesting in rocky holes and crevasses on the hillside and the cormorants were nesting on the sheer cliffs above. I was listening with interest at what the lads were saying to each other, and the balustrade guy said "How do you tell the difference between a shag and a cormorant?" and his mate said, "Well John, that's probably why you're still a bachelor, mate."

We had lots of fun and it was a very successful cruise. I still have that newspaper feature to this very day, but it looks quite old and yellow now.

Coming back from Barra in the Outer Hebrides with five guests on board one day, the weather took a turn for the worse, and hit us completely by surprise. I was heading for Arinagour on the Isle of Coll and it was blowing force seven gusting eight. The waves were crashing on my starboard quarter, so this was going to be a really rough, wet trip. As soon as I had got the sails reefed, I sent everyone below and was sailing as close to the wind as this boat could manage, which meant it was going to be a very bumpy and wet sail. The waves came right over the bows and into the cockpit, good thing it was self-draining. I endured this for hours, can't remember how many. What I can remember was saying to myself "If I make it back to dry land, I'm never going out again".

When I finally arrived and anchored in the bay, my guests came out and started laughing at me. The chef said, "You should look at your face". It was white with salt crystals, with two blood-red eyes peering out.

Two pints in the pub later and I was planning our next port of call. After two years of one-week sailing trips with me, John the bank manager asked me if I would do a sixteen-day cruise and I said "Yes, I can do that, John" so he booked the boat for three weeks. Because there were no other bookings for that length of time, I invited a mate to help out as it was going to be a long journey. We intended to sail to all the inner Hebridean Islands and along the entire length of the outer Hebridean chain of Islands.

We set off up the sound of Mull and around Ardnamurchan Point, then across to the islands of Muck and Eigg, briefly visiting each one, then on to the Isle of Rum, where we spent the night in Loch Scresort. We had a lovely visit to the island of Soay, where Gavin Maxwell, the author of *Ring of Bright Water*, worked with his friend in their attempt to create a basking shark fishery. We met his friend's wife, whose husband was the owner of the shark oil processing plant. It was still there but in a dilapidated condition and no longer used, and the massive round tanks which held the oil were now rusted through. He was away on business, so we never got to meet him but had tea in their cottage with his charming wife. We passed under dozens of items of clothing hanging from the ceiling to dry, and we had to bend low to get under them and into the sitting room. It was a very homely atmosphere overlooking the beautiful bay and the Cuillin Sound.

After a very memorable visit and a promise to return, we continued our journey round the point of Sleat into the Sound of Sleat and through the Kyle of Rhea, a very dangerous tidal stream only passable by using the engine flat out. Clearing the Kyle of Lochalsh with its strong currents, we were now in the Inner Sound and heading for our next port of call. We were now heading for Lochinver, passing the Summer Isles and a small island called Gruinard Island. There are notices all around the island warning everyone not to set foot on its soil. This was where the MOD experimented with anthrax for chemical warfare during the war years and it was still very contaminated (it was finally given a clean bill of health in 1990). I gave it a wide berth. We particularly sailed to Lochinver as the son of Alison, our on-board cordon bleu chef, had just taken up a job at the hotel as a commis chef and we went to visit him.

Next day was Sunday. I had set a course for Stornoway on the Isle of Lewis when half-way across the Minch, John reminded me the people of Lewis were very religious and look down on any activities taking place on a Sunday such as sailing. I respected their traditions and altered course to the Shiant Islands, a small group of islands almost in the centre of the Minch. The largest island has a wee cottage on the top of a hill. When we were there, three men stood just outside the cottage door looking at us all the time we were there, which must have been two hours at least. We began to think they must be statues as they never altered their positions; they just kept on watching us, but we didn't go ashore.

Our next overnight stay was on Harris, where we found a nice sheltered anchorage and checked out the village and the history of the lovely Harris Tweed cloth and yes, I do have a Harris Tweed jacket. The night wasn't to be as peaceful as we thought, as on a little flat grassy island near where we were anchored a colony of Arctic terns were nesting. Running around this island was a mink, and every now and then it would run out of its crevice in the rock, snatch a baby bird from a nest and run back through the colony, sending the terns screeching and dive bombing. This went on throughout the night, bearing in mind that it doesn't get dark at this time of year in Scotland.

John was enjoying his cruise very much and he was continually making notes and observing things. I asked him why all the notes, what were they for? He said that when he was permanently back in the UK his ambition was to write and publish a West of Scotland sailing guide based on his many years sailing these waters. One of the main reasons he sailed on my boat so often was that I visited out of the way places where most charter yachts never went, mostly because I had a shallow draft.

From Harris we sailed the rest of the Hebridean Isles taking in points of interest. At about South Uist we ran into very dense sea fog. I knew that if I kept to my planned compass bearing there were no off-shore dangers, but the trouble with fog is there's usually no wind, so that meant motoring.

We came across a stationary yacht and saw people on

it standing waving at us, so I motored over to them and shouted "Are you all right?"

"We are completely lost," the skipper shouted

"Where are you heading for?" I shouted.

"Lochboisdale." We were quite close to them now so we didn't have to shout. I could see he was really worried, so I broke the ice by having a little chuckle and said, "You've just passed it."

"No!" he said in surprise

"Follow me, I'm going past it and I'll show you where to turn off."

I altered my course and headed in towards the land until I could just see it. You have to know these waters, because in these conditions when you're passing a loch entrance the land disappears from view and you can become disorientated. I arrived at the entrance, waited for him and showed him where to go, but he came right alongside, and I wondered what he was doing. One of his crew members was trying to pass over a bottle of wine as a thank you gift, and of course I accepted it – it was Blossom Hill, one of my favourite wines. I told him where to go, he thanked me several times and we carried on our journey, stopping the night at Barra, where we managed to get some fish and chips.

Next day the fog had cleared and we set off for the island of Mingulay, a jewel of an island, extremely remote and the most southerly island of the Outer Hebrides, apart from a rock just south of Mingulay called Barra Head. Mingulay once had a small community in a little village on the edge of a sandy beach, but unfortunately the beach has almost buried what's left of it with windblown sand. It has been uninhabited for many years. They must have been a hardy folk living there with the might of the whole Atlantic roaring past in all directions. The short time we were there was quite humbling. There was a sort of latent tension, like trying not to wake something up; we all felt it, like being on borrowed time. The sea was silently filling up the whole bay and then sighing as it retreated out again.

We did make time to visit the puffins on the grass-covered cliffs and marvelled at their antics, they are so friendly. I would love to have stayed a night here in the bay but it's not a recommended anchorage, unfortunately.

Now we had a long sail ahead of us and would be out of sight of land for a few hours. The sea was calm and the wind light, but enough to sail by. After about an hour there was a wonderful smell of baking bread and cooked turkey wafting up from the galley, and everyone got quite excited about it. Alison the chef was performing her magic once again. The reason we always had turkey on or near the last day of the cruise was that on stocking the boat ready for a cruise, we put a large frozen turkey in the big cool box which kept all the other stuff cool, and by the time we were ready to cook it, usually after about a week, it had thawed out and was ready to cook. This worked very well.

One day we sailed into a swarm of massive jellyfish – some of them must have been five or six feet long including their tentacles, and they looked like what you might think alien spaceships would look like. They must have been ocean-going jellyfish as I had never seen them in inshore waters before. I have since learnt they are called barrel jellyfish, the biggest found in British waters, and they do occasionally get washed up onshore en masse.

Lunch was taken sitting in the cockpit. It was nice and warm, the wind was behind us and I was flying my one thousand square-foot cruising chute, which was finding wind we could not even feel. A small bird landed on the deck; I think it was a wagtail, and it must have been exhausted, for it was soon asleep with its head tucked under its wing. It stayed with us for quite some time until land came into sight, when the bird shook itself, strutted around the deck and took off to resume its journey.

On the horizon I could just make out the hilltop on Tiree, so I plotted a course for the Gunna Sound, a passage between Coll and Tiree. Our next stop was Arinagour on Coll, where we would spend the night. There was a very nice hotel pub on Coll which I had visited many times. My guests and I would add our names and comments in the logbook at the bar every time we visited the island. Arinagour was always a favourite anchorage of mine; it has good anchor-holding ground and I have sat out many a storm there.

Next day, having had a good night in the pub and a long walk, we set off on the west side of the Isle of Mull to visit the Treshnish Isles and the Isle of Staffa with a quick visit to Fingal's cave and then on through the Sound of Iona to Oban, passing Colonsay and the Garvellachs.

I dropped John off at Oban, where he had left his car, and the rest of the crew came back with me to Taynuilt. John continued to come each year to sail with me and we visited many more out-of-the-way places, the like of which the normal charter yachts never go to, mainly because of their deep draught.

An interesting charter I had was with an Austrian family on board, father, mother with three gorgeous daughters, and I fancied all three. The guy was quite a character and was up for any adventure, but his wife spent most of the time in her cabin drinking wine. I got the impression she was not there of her own choosing. Now I didn't mind that, but what upset me most was that she never offered me a drink, ever.

For the first dinner on board, we were anchored in Little Horseshoe Bay on the Isle of Kerrera. This is another of my favourite anchorages, it's close to Oban and by the time I had met guests from the train and got them on board, it was just a short sail before it was time for dinner. This particular meal was grilled rainbow trout and the wine was an up-and-coming English white wine I had read about in a magazine, so thought I'd give it a try. Well the meal didn't go down very well at all. Straightaway they said "Where are the heads? The fish haven't any heads," they all said as a chorus.

"The chef cuts them off when she guts them," I explained.

"But we like to eat the head, the eyes are my favourite," one of the girls said.

"Ho, I didn't know that I'm sorry," I said as I poured the wine.

The wife had one sip and went off to fetch her own wine. "I didn't think the English made wine," she said, almost knowledgeably. The husband gave her a stony look and then he tried the wine. I could tell that he didn't like it either, but he put on a brave face. They didn't drink it, but I did and thought it was rather nice.

I remember one time when I sailed to Craignure on the Isle of Mull, two of the crew were girls on holiday. We were anchored in the bay and the tide was in, so getting out of the dinghy at the pier was quite easy, just a few rungs of an iron ladder then a short walk to the pub. It was a beautiful evening and we had a great time chatting to the locals. After a jolly good time, we all headed off to the pier to go aboard the yacht. The tide by now had gone out, which meant we had to climb down a long, slippery metal ladder. I was the first to descend to get the dinghy ready, but just as I had stepped into it one of the girls fell past me and into the sea, missing me and the boat by a fraction of an inch. She scrambled into the dinghy with my help. Luckily she wasn't hurt, just very wet, and she was still giggling. I said "There's an easier way of getting in the dinghy, you know." She was the smaller of the two girls and quite bonny. We boarded the yacht and soon after she complained she was having difficulty breathing and she needed to change into dry clothing. The petticoat-style fine leather jacket she was wearing had shrunk, and she could not undo the little buttons running down the front of the garment – there were many of them and it was getting tighter. Her friend decided it would have to be cut off. I found her some scissors and stood back in anticipation. It was so tight she could hardly get the scissors under it.

Three or four button loops were cut, and the jacket was taking on a very strange shape, then suddenly it blew – first one button flew off, then a series of them one after the other, a bit like a machine gun or something out of a comedy show. Everything burst open. There was a loud inhalation of breath and she fell on her knees, which was just as well to preserve her own modesty, as her dress and blouse were transparent from being wet. One of the younger guys standing by just couldn't turn away – I honestly thought his eyes were going to pop out.

I quickly gave her a blanket and she went to her cabin to change. After a short time, she reappeared in her usual happy-go-lucky way, full of smiles, downed a nice big gin and tonic and she was ready to party once again, bless her.

With the weather being very nice for a change and with suitable guests as crew, I decided to visit the island of St Kilda, forty miles west of the Outer Hebrides. It's only accessible in a boat this size during good weather. There is only one anchorage out there and that's Village Bay, on the main island. I picked my way through the Sound of Harris and its seemingly millions of rocks – exaggeration of course – and anchored just off Berneray to await the shipping forecast. It warned of a deepening depression moving rapidly in from the west with gale to severe gales later. Well that was that then – by the time we got there the weather would be upon us and that was not the sort of place you want to be in bad weather. I told the crew this and we aborted the idea and decided to go ashore and comb the beach for tropical seeds. I have found these in the past; they are very hard-shelled and beautiful. Some are a perfect heart shape with a dark mahogany colour about the size of a golf ball, while some are round, flattish and black. I still have them apart from the heart-shaped one, which I gave away.

I launched the dinghy and we rowed ashore, but just as we reached the sandy beach a large wave hit the stern of the dinghy and swung it around. A female guest was caught unprepared and she lost her camera overboard, along with all her precious photos. I really felt sorry for her. I was able to retrieve it, but unfortunately the damage was done by the ingress of salt water. On this occasion we never found any seeds, but as usual it was lovely to walk on the machair, the fertile calcareous grassland found in this region, amid all the wonderful wild flowers. We visited the small village, but strangely no one seemed to be there. I carried on the cruise, calling at all the usual places.

I went on to do many more sailing trips, averaging about three thousand nautical miles per season, covering the whole of the Inner and Outer Hebrides. Most were just plain sailing with nothing much to report.

Chapter 14

Treading the boards

~~~~~~~~

It was now around 1988, and Mike and I found ourselves co-opted into the Oban Operatic Society. I'm not going to say why, because it's somewhat embarrassing, needless to say. I made a promise to turn up at a rehearsal in Oban and dragged Mike along with me. He was saying "But... but..." and I just replied, "No buts, you're coming."

They were rehearsing for a musical called *Free as Air*, and our parts were in the background with minor roles, Mike was given a small row-on part as the ferryman and I had a walk-on part and was a member of the chorus. With only weeks to go before the opening in Oban at the Corran Halls, one of the principal actors had to pull out through ill health, and with no one to take his place the musical director, who was also my neighbour at that time and the reason I was there in the first place, asked if I would step in and take on the role. I agreed and then got instant butterflies in my stomach. What have I done, I wondered to myself?

I was to play the part of Mr. Potter the bailiff. Over the coming weeks I managed to learn my libretto and the songs. Then came the big night and it all went very well except towards the end. Earlier, Mike had asked a mate of his from Glasgow, who was staying locally, if he would help with the scenery back stage and he proved to be very good, but what we didn't know was that he had smuggled a bottle of whisky backstage and hid it in the dressing room toilet flushing system, and every now and then he would go and have a dram. Very soon it was notable how unsteady he was getting, falling about the stage and giggling. There was a massive stage flat of Miss Catamole's house, which was a main feature. It occupied most of the stage and she very nearly ended up wearing it. Mike's friend backstage had fallen onto it and we managed to catch it only just in time. He was banished from the set instantly and Mike got a right old bollocking for bringing him in the first place.

I got a taste for acting and went on to do other parts, for instance in 1990 I played the part of Curly in the musical *Oklahoma* by Rodgers & Hammerstein. I think I got the part because I was the only guy there who had enough hair to curl. My counterpart, Jud Fry, was played by a guy called Del, an elderly man who had a fantastic singing voice and often sang at weddings and parties. Two nights before the show he turned up for rehearsal without any teeth in, which of course affected his singing voice as well as his appearance, which didn't really go with the role of a young, strong cowboy. I thought the director was going to have a meltdown. "What the bloody hell are we going to do?" she said. As the baddie, Jud Fry, he had a principal part in this production, but he looked like he was all mouth and lips. I asked him "Where are your teeth, Del?"

"Well, you're not going to believe this," he said and he started to tell me what had happened. "I went to the toilet and you know how you stand there holding the chain while you pee?"

"No Del, I never do that" I interrupted him.

"Well, I was standing there and I had a sudden coughing fit, and my teeth shot out into the toilet bowl just as I pulled the chain by mistake, it was an involuntary jerk reaction. I ran outside and lifted the manhole cover, but they had gone," he said with an upward gesture of his hands.

"Can you get any more?"

"Don't think so, not enough time to get a set made."

"Have you tried the antique shops? They sometimes have old teeth." Del did turn up on the night with a full set of ivories. They looked very big, very white and sparkling and he could only just close his mouth. Where he got them from I have no idea and he wouldn't say. The show went on and was a great success, apart from one incident which was when I fired my pistol. It made such a loud bang that it momentarily took out the whole sound system.

I did lots of amateur acting roles over those early years, and played just about everything. If they needed someone old and ugly, I got the part. In the pantomime Cinderella, a mate and I played the part of the two ugly sisters. I went to a lot of trouble fashioning a pair of old knickers by putting lead shot around the seams, to make them heavy enough to fall when I pulled a short string, as I thought it would get a good laugh. The show was in the local Taynuilt village hall, and we were in front of the curtain singing the song 'Sisters' when suddenly the audience started laughing and I couldn't understand why. My co-star also started suppressing his laughter and his eyes kept looking up at the top of my head. Then I felt it – the curtain was made of synthetic material which was setting up an electrostatic charge in my blonde wig, causing it to stream upwards and eventually lifting it off my head. We did a little jig and went through the curtain, then an arm sneaked out from behind the curtain and grabbed the wig, which was not rehearsed. At the end of the show we walked on stage to take our bow – this was when I had wanted to do my knicker-dropping stunt. Well it worked perfectly, but the problem was that the audience was sitting lower than the stage so they never saw it. Only one guy who was standing at the back saw it, and he roared with laughter and everyone in the audience turned to look at him.

Chapter 15

More adventures

~~~~~

One winter, Mike and I decided we could do with a little adventure, as it was early February and a slack time for me as far as yacht chartering was concerned. We planned a sail to Benbecula in the Outer Hebrides. We did all the necessary preparations and on a fine and pleasant day we set off.

Our first port of call was the small island of Canna, one of a group of islands in the Inner Hebrides. It was mid-afternoon when we dropped anchor just outside the tiny harbour so Mike could have a dive to see if he could get any king scallops for supper – he had brought all his diving gear on board. He came up with about two dozen of the biggest scallops I had ever seen, at that time of my life anyway – most of them were over six inches across. We had a lovely early supper and a few drinks, then it was time to go ashore and see if we could make a phone call.

As we were walking along the harbour road, Mike suddenly said "Do you think we should pose as visiting curates?"

"What! Are you insane?" I replied. "Just look at yourself, you have enough food down your jumper to feed a small village, odd socks, pants you've just worn under your dive suit, a cheap camouflage jacket and you're half pissed. I would hardly think you're dressed for the part. Just because there are two churches on here does not make us men of the cloth."

There wasn't a soul to be seen, and the place looked and felt deserted. We soon came to the one and only phone box. It was the old-fashioned press A and B buttons type box, and you had to put eighty pence in before you got a line. Had we got eighty pence in change? No. We were just about to head back to the boat when a woman suddenly appeared, and she seemed surprised when she saw us. "Goodness me" she said, "what are you two doing here this time of year?"

Mike began to say "Well, we are visiting…" before I cut him off.

"We are just visiting, staying the night and heading for the Outer Hebrides in the morning," I said. "We were trying to make a phone call but couldn't find the change."

"Oh, don't bother with that old thing, come into the

shop there's a phone in there." Then as she looked out of the window at the yacht she added, "Nobody sails here in the winter months." Inside there was a modern phone, and she said "Help yourself, I have a few things to attend to while I'm here." We made our calls, bought a bottle of whisky, said thank you very much, wished her good night and headed back to the boat.

Next day there was an absolute pea-souper. Visibility was down to about five yards and to make things worse, according to the Admiralty charts there was a compass abnormality on the island of Canna affecting the sea area. I charted a course taking into consideration the magnetic deviation of the massive chunk of granite that was Canna. We did not have all the fancy satellite navigation plotters they have on boats these days; all navigation was done using a compass, parallel rules, Admiralty charts of the sea area we were sailing in, a bit of dead reckoning, a lot of eyeball navigation and that was it. I did try my hand at astral navigation but didn't take to it much at all, as it was far too cloudy most of the time.

We soon got under way, heading for the outer marker buoy just off Benbecula. There was little or no wind, so most of the time we were motoring with just the mainsail up, which gave us a little help by giving us an apparent wind, in other words we were making our own wind by using the engine – it's a bit complicated but it works.

Sailing across the Sea of the Hebrides at about six or seven knots was going to take the best part of the day. The fog never lifted at all. Eventually I told Mike to look out for the outer marker buoy and wow, there she was, I almost hit it. "What about that for navigation?" I shouted to Mike. "Aaaar, not bad" he replied. We anchored just off the pier at Peter's Port.

Next day the fog had lifted, but it was replaced by a strengthening wind and a north-westerly severe storm force twelve forecast coming in later. We decided to go ashore while we could, get some provisions and go to the Creagorry pub, which is in the Guinness Book of Records for selling the largest amount of whisky in a single night.

After doing our shopping we visited people we knew on the island, especially 'Supergran', as we called her. She had got the name on an earlier visit to the island when we met her coming out of the Co-Op with two huge bags. I immediately offered to take her bags. "Bloody hell!" I said. I could hardly lift them, and she would have carried them all the way home, over a mile, hence the name.

It was early evening before we got to the pub, and it looked like everyone was already celebrating. We took a small table away from the bar and had a pint or two watching the antics of the locals. They looked like professional drinkers all right. As the night wore on, we moved to the bar and sat on bar stools, and I spotted this big girl making a beeline straight for me from across a crowded smoky pub. She almost knocked me off my stool trying to sit on my knee "Where do you come from then?" she enquired in a slurring voice.

"The mainland," I said. She had arms like thighs and was one of the girls who worked in the fish processing factory, I was later told.

"My husband is through there," she said, pointing to some French doors. "Oh shit, that's all I bloody need," I thought, pushing her over to Mike. No sooner had I got her off my knee when the doors flung open and there was her man, holding both doors open as he scanned the crowd for his wife. He saw her on Mike's knee and set off towards her. He held a glass of whisky in one hand and both arms and legs were splayed out from his body as he walked stiff-legged towards the bar. He never spilled a drop of whisky, but when he got about two yards from us he went down flat on his face and spilled his whisky all down his wife. A couple of guys picked him up and carted him off through the doors he had come in from; I got the impression it was a regular occurrence. His wife mopped herself up with a handkerchief, strutted off with some of her mates and that was it, time for us to go. There was a taxi's phone number on a card pinned to a notice board, so I rang it, and sure enough a taxi came.

"Where to, lads?" he said.

"Peter's Port pier" I said and off we went.

On arrival we could see that the Sea of the Hebrides was white with breaking waves. The taxi shone his headlights towards the boat, which was pitching, tossing and rolling. I said to Mike, "It looks like a night sleeping in the dinghy under the pier." If we had attempted to go out to the boat, we would have been blown out to sea.

The taxi driver got out of the car and said, "There's no way you can get out there to your boat lads, you had better come back with me and we'll have another look in a couple of hours". The storm had hit earlier than was expected so we thought, but this was not the real storm – that was still to come – this was just a preliminary strong wind before the storm.

Back at the taxi man's house (I am sorry I can't remember his name, he gave me a card and I kept it for years but it's lost in the passage of time, though he will know who it is if he ever reads this) he brought out beer and whisky and asked if we wanted anything to eat. I said "That's very kind of you, but we don't want to put you to any trouble". We settled for a beer and soon his wife came in with a plate full of sandwiches.

At about midnight he drove us back to the boat; there wasn't any change, in fact it was worse. He took us back to his house and we had another beer or two and then bedded down in the armchairs. In the morning, after a fantastic breakfast, he took us back to the boat and it was calm enough to row out. We thanked him very much and asked him "How much do we owe you?"

He said "Well boys, I will have to charge you two pounds". Mike and I looked at each other. We only had ten pounds between us and we gave it to him. He went in his pocket for change and we had a little smile. "No, keep it all" I said.

Back on board I checked for any damage. The real storm was yet to come, so I let out all the anchor chain I had and went onto my Marlow 18mm Multiplat anchor warp.

The storm hit in the early hours of the morning, and the noise was horrendous. My masthead anemometer went off the clock at sixty knots, and the pointer was pressed hard against the stop all the time. I had noted the jagged metal hull of a half-submerged shipwreck about forty yards astern of me and had visions of my anchor warp parting and us being blown onto the wreck. My beautiful shiny GRP hull would not stand a chance against the rusty lacerations of the wreck.

The shipping forecast did nothing to calm my nerves "Malin, Hebrides, Minch, violent storm eleven increasing hurricane storm twelve" - that's hurricane force. Oh shit, another sleepless night. There was nothing we could do but ride it out. Mike went off to his cabin and soon after I could hear sleep sounds. I must have nodded off myself, as when I awoke I couldn't see out of the forward window, so at first light I was up on deck. The wind had abated somewhat but not a lot, and the forward deck was smothered by at least a foot of seaweed, kelp and bladderwrack, and there was even a large piece of thick green fishing net. The high winds and big tides had washed it from the shoreline, completely covering the windows. At first I wondered how it had come aboard, but then I realised it had blown up the anchor warp.

The wind blew at gale force all day. At about six o'clock the taxi man turned up at the pier flashing his headlights and shouting "Do you want to go to the pub?" but the sea state was still too rough for our little dinghy, so I declined his offer.

Overnight the wind died down quite a lot, but according to the shipping forecast there were more deep depressions in the Atlantic waiting to come in. This was the time to head back home, where there was more shelter from the pending storms. I went forward to weigh anchor, but it was easier said than done, as the anchor had buried itself six foot into the thick, dense grey mud and it took two of us all our strength to get it on board. We could tell how deep it had dug itself in by the mud caked on the chain. We had to be quick about it though, as we were drifting backwards towards the wreck once the anchor was free. Now, with a favourable wind in our sails, we could fly across the Sea of The Hebrides at an average speed of fourteen knots, reaching twenty plus at times. Our adventure had been cut short, but I was sure there would be more to come.

My yacht chartering business was not doing as well as I had hoped. I did not get enough charters to sustain me through the winter months and had to look elsewhere. Then I saw an ad in the local newspaper; a film company was looking for extras for a film called *Local Hero*. I rang them up and got an interview at Fort William, so off I went. I found the hotel and was surprised to see so many other potential actors all waiting in line to be interviewed.

My turn came, and I faced the small panel of men and a woman sitting at a table. The main guy asked if I could ride a motorbike and I said yes. They took my photo with a polaroid camera, wrote my name and address on the back of it and that was it, they paid me some expenses and off I went.

Still looking for something to do I saw another ad, for someone with experience repairing boats. The pay was OK, so I contacted them and we arranged a day, time and place to meet. I was told to go to the Morar Hotel near Mallaig. I arrived early afternoon and sat in the bar area having a cup of tea. Just as I had finished my tea there was a frighteningly loud noise outside, windows rattled and the ground trembled. The barman said "There's a helicopter just landed in the carpark," and people got up to look out of the windows.

I was about to have a look myself when a bloke opened the door, leaned in and shouted "Mr Rockley?" I immediately put my hand up just like a school child and obediently followed him out, as did everyone else for that matter. He took my upper arm and ran me, head bowed, to the helicopter. There was quite a crowd gathered and I felt a bit like James Bond. When the taking-off noise had quietened somewhat, I shouted to the guy, who happened to be the big boss, "Why the helicopter?"

He replied, "Where we are going there aren't any roads. The only way in is to walk, fly or boat, and that's where you come in, we need a safe boat."

We landed near an old but well-built pier, and I saw a dozen or more 45-gallon oil drums, helicopter fuel I thought. He showed me where the boat was moored, alongside a jetty in the mouth of the river Meoble. We had a good long chat, and he showed me around the place and the little cottage where I was to stay. I then flew back to the hotel car park with just the pilot.

After a couple of days' preparation for the job in hand, I got a letter from the film company with a load of instructions as to where to go and so on, but I had made a commitment and that was it – pity, because I did fancy an acting part in a film.

Alison, a friend and I sailed up to Loch Nevis and anchored in a little bay. The sea chart warned that the ground could be foul, which meant I could get my anchor snagged on a sunken wreck or something, so I put down an anchor trip rope attached to a small buoy. Big mistake. We started cooking a large turkey, and when it was about half cooked the helicopter turned up to take us over Loch Morar – he had arrived earlier than we expected. I was anchored opposite a small white cottage near the loch in about fifty foot of water. The bay was like a large underwater bowl, which made it a good place for anchoring, especially in onshore winds.

We rowed ashore carrying the turkey wrapped in aluminium foil, hoping we could carry on cooking it at the wee cottage. I tied up my dinghy well above the high tide mark. The helicopter had landed on the beach and there was a very strong gusting wind, which was of great concern to the pilot, who was shouting to us to be as quick as we could to get on board.

An old gentleman had come out of the little cottage to see what was going on, and we introduced ourselves. He was Donald MacDonald, a lovely chap. I asked him if he would keep an eye on my boat and dinghy. "Oh, don't worry about that" he said, and that made me feel a lot better about leaving them. The wind blew the tin foil covering off the turkey as we were getting into the helicopter and the old man couldn't believe his eyes. He shouted something, but of course we couldn't hear him.

When we arrived at the Meoble estate, which was many thousands of acres (I was told how many but I've forgotten exactly) and miles from anywhere, we set about checking out my wee cottage. It was very basic with only one bedroom, a large settee, a gas cooker and a sink against the wall in the kitchen. For electricity there was a generator called a Start-a-matic, in very common use throughout remote areas of the Highlands. It was in a tiny shed about a hundred yards away from the cottage. It hadn't been run for God knows how long and was supposed to be an automatic start, but the car battery that started it had seen better days. I gave it a service and got the diesel engine working using a manual hand crank, but not the auto start. This meant that when we switched the last light out in the cottage, the generator stopped and we had to go to the shed to start it again manually if we wanted to switch a light on.

The first day I went to the boat I was there to repair, I met the boss. I must admit the boat looked like the *African Queen* and was just about as old. It was sitting on the riverbed, full of water. It had a clinker-built hull, which needed one hell of a lot of work including caulking and the replacement of several planks. I said to the boss, "You can't do what needs to be done on this boat while it's in the water, it needs lifting out and putting in that big shed, and I bet it weighs about eight ton. It's past its sell by date."

"Oh dear" he said, "we don't have a crane or any other way of getting it out onto dry land. Perhaps you can have a look at this other boat, it's the one we are using now." The other one was quite a good solid glass fibre work vessel with a decent diesel inboard engine. The problem was that the deck had broken away from the hull in quite a few places, thus greatly restricting the amount of weight she could carry. It was a self-draining deck, but because of the damage the water now flooded into the engine compartment. I suspected the reason for the damage was dropping those forty-five-gallon oil drums onto the deck, as I could see evidence of it.

"I can fix that if I can get hold of the materials and of course, dry warm weather," I told him.

"Very good, I'm so pleased to hear that," he said. "There's a chandlery in Mallaig, they sell all that kind of stuff. I will organise it and you can get what you want, the estate has an account there." Alison and a mate named Brian had to get back to their own routines, having only stayed one night, and they had a good feast of the turkey, but there was enough for me to pick on later. They had to walk out through woodland and over some substantial hilly terrain and I accompanied them; it took the best part of a day. Alison got these nasty keds on her eyelids, there were dozens of them and they had clamped her eyes shut. I had to pull them off as quickly as I could, as they are a parasitic fly which normally feed on deer. It was a long walk out to the road where they were able to catch a bus to Fort William, and I saw them off and ran all the way back so as to beat the pending darkness.

Over the next few days I managed to get into Mallaig and got all the items I required for fixing the boat. All I needed now was some dry weather and warmer temperatures. It rained every day for a solid week, but I was able to do some preparations to the hull and deck with the aid of an old canvas sheet shelter over me.

I soon began to realise just how remote I was. There was a worry about getting food, and with the supply I had brought with me almost gone, I was supplementing my diet with blackberries and wild mushrooms (I class myself as a bit of an expert on wild fungi). Scrounging around in one of the sheds I came across some fishing tackle, which was just what I needed, so I did some spinning for trout. This place must have been a hive of activity at some time, judging by the amount of stuff in the sheds. I had no luck at all spinning, so I decided to try the old-fashioned way, worm, that will get 'em, I thought. I followed the river upstream to where there was a back flow on a bend in the river, started digging with my knife for a worm and shifted half the riverbank before I found one. I had soon hooked a beauty, but as I was about to get it onto the sloping bank it flipped off and rolled back in and was gone. This happened three times and each time I had to go through the digging routine for a worm. I tried different sized hooks and was getting quite desperate.

The fourth fish was a big one, so I swung it way onto the bank and dived on it, determined that this one would not get away. I picked it up and ran towards the cottage when it was suddenly snatched from my grasp. Oh shit! Of course it was still attached to the rod and line. I ate well that night.

Still waiting for a change in the weather, I went exploring. This place was so wild. Two ravens were mobbing a golden eagle and were pushing their luck. The eagle turned on its back and caught one of the ravens a glancing blow with its talons. There was an explosion of black feathers and the raven got the message. It flew off in a dead straight line followed by its mate, away from the eagle and potential death.

In a fold of the land, completely remote and out of sight, I came across a small building. It was in very good condition, and judging by the brambles blocking the doorway and windows, it hadn't been visited in a long time. The door wasn't locked, so I went in after smashing the brambles out of the way with a stick. I couldn't believe my eyes. It was a school, complete with desks, about six or seven, lots of chalk, a blackboard and on each desk was a slate in a wooden frame for writing on with the chalk, as well as lots of children's books. There were kids' paintings pinned on the walls, everything you would expect to see in a kids' school – it was just like stepping back in time. They must have left suddenly and never gone back. It was kind of strange seeing this as there were no houses there at all apart from the big estate house almost two miles up a very rough dirt track, which was occupied by a very pleasant lady who was responsible for paying me. The boss didn't live there – he came and went in his helicopter. He owned the place but lived in Ireland.

I desperately needed to check out my yacht sitting at anchor in Loch Nevis, and I couldn't take the big boat, which had to remain where it was in case of emergency. Rummaging through one of the sheds I found two Seagull outboard motors, a small one and a much bigger one. They are advertised as being the most reliable outboard there is, but that's not quite true as I couldn't get a spark out of either of them. On a shelf I found a box covered in dust and cobwebs with a picture of a man carrying a Seagull outboard on his shoulder, and found that it was an overhaul kit for the small engine, all wrapped in green greaseproof paper, I fitted it and got it going.

All I needed now was a boat. I found a couple of small boats which were abandoned and looking quite sad. I turned over the best looking of the two, a clinker rowing boat about six or seven feet long, a very small boat for going across Loch Morar. But oh dear, I am afraid it had seen better days. In the water it leaked from just about every plank. I fixed it up the best I could and left it in the water to see if it would swell the planks more. The next day was much better, the sun shone and it wasn't raining, so I got cracking on repairing the big boat. If I got just a few more days like this I could get it finished, and as it turned out I did, and the boat was ready. The key to glass fibre is getting a good chemical bond at the right temperature, so preparation of the old glass fibre is very important and you need a good supply of acetone.

I was invited up to the big house for dinner, which was just as well as I was out of food. The boss was there and a couple of other people I had not met before – they must have flown in by helicopter. It was a lovely meal with a nice glass of wine. When it was time to go it was pitch black outside, so I borrowed a powerful torch and set off. About halfway I stood still and shone the torch in a circle around me. On my right-hand side facing down the track, there were dozens of bright red eyes staring at me, deer, and on my left, there was one pair of bright green eyes. "What the hell is that?" I said out loud. I picked up a stone and threw it at the eyes. They disappeared for a second or two, but then they were back and I thought they were closer to me than before. I made as much noise as I possibly could by kicking stones and gravel as I walked.

On reflection, I remembered that two days previously I was heading back to my cottage when in the distance I spotted a cat-like creature walking up the track, a fair distance from me. It was a cat, with a sandy mottled appearance, but the strange thing about it was its gait; its front legs at the shoulder seemed to protrude above the sides of its body, like a lion or cougar. It was hard to tell how big this cat was. I knew there were a lot of wildcats around, but I was sure it was not wildcat size. I wondered if this was the animal whose eyes I had seen and I had disturbed it hunting the deer. I never saw its face, but it was its walk that was most puzzling. Anyway I didn't hang around. I hot-footed it to my little cottage as quickly as I could and locked the door.

The next day was a good time for me to go and check my boat. I set off about lunchtime with the Seagull engine fitted to the rowing boat and an old pair of oars just in case. There was a slight swirling mist over the loch, and I hoped it wouldn't get any worse. Very soon it was evident that I would have to do a lot of bailing out of water, and going across seemed to take forever; the engine was spluttering badly and stopped a couple of times. I put the oars out to row, but after only a few strokes half the paddle blade broke off one of the oars, which was trying to make me row in a circle. Rowing made me neglect bailing and the leaking was getting worse, time to have another go at the engine. I got it going again, but it would only run at a very slow rate.

I could just make out the other side of the loch, but I couldn't see where I had come from, I must have been over halfway when I remembered that Loch Morar is one of the deepest lochs in Scotland and has its own monster lurking around down there, so they say. A shiver ran down my spine; better be as quiet as I can I thought. I must admit I felt very lonely and vulnerable out there in a sinking boat with a dodgy engine, one and a half paddles and with no one knowing I was doing this.

On arrival I pulled the dinghy up onto dry land and tied it up, then climbed up the steep hill and looked down to see my boat through a gap in the mountains to Loch Nevis. "Wow, I could just do with a pint after all that," I said to myself. On getting aboard I checked everything and it was fine, so I weighed anchor and sailed across Loch Nevis to Knoydart, where I knew there was a community-type pub. I had about three pints, enjoyed a chat with the locals, sailed back to the bay, dropped the anchor along with its trip rope and went to my bunk, job done.

Next morning, I spluttered the little boat back to Meoble and put it behind the shed for protection. I made some finishing touches to the big boat and that was me all finished.

Finally got to the shop in the village of Morar and stocked up on food, even though I knew I would not be there much longer – well, two days to be exact. I had finished the boat in the nick of time as the nights were turning bitterly cold. The wee cottage had no insulation, just thick stone walls which acted as cold radiators, so a fire was called for. What little wood there was for burning was wet through, but the tubes of mastic I was given to caulk the boat with and hadn't used burnt very well for a long time and gave off a lot of heat. I was sure the fumes would be carcinogenic if I breathed them in for long periods.

The weather had turned cold, wet and quite windy; there was nothing there for me to do, so I went to the big house to report my progress and hopefully get paid. They were very pleased with what I had done and gave me fifty pounds extra as a thank you gesture. I also got permission to take two jerry cans of aviation fuel from the drum, which had been punctured, as they would not use it in case it had been contaminated with water. I made a second trip to the yacht to take the fuel, tools and personal things and generally ready the yacht for my departure and have a pint or two at the pub. The crossing was just as scary as last time, but at least I had got the engine running much better, so it only took about half the time to get across the Loch although my heart did skip a beat or two when I spotted a very large black shape off my starboard side, thankfully it turned out to be a tree trunk.

When I got to the top of the mountain pass and looked down to where my yacht should have been anchored in the little bay, I saw to my horror and disbelief that it wasn't there; the bay was empty. I don't remember coming down that mountain pass with two jerry cans of fuel a task I had been dreading, all kinds of thoughts were going through my mind. If it was sunk the mast would still be visible. I was distraught, then I realised I was still carrying the fuel such was my state of mind.

I checked the dinghy, which was still there tied up where I had left it. The next thing I was knocking on the old man's door, and it seemed like forever before he answered. When he did, he was quite excited and couldn't get the words out quick enough. "Oh, there you are" he said, breathing out heavily. I felt like shouting "Where the hell is my yacht?" but he quickly said "Your boat is safe, it's at Tom McClean's adventure centre just a wee way down the Loch." I felt a wave of relief sweep over me but I was still very worried.

"What happened to it?" I enquired.

"It dragged its anchor and was drifting out of the bay, so Tom and his men towed it to his pontoon." I knew I should never have left that trip rope on the anchor when I wasn't on board. The buoy at low water had wound itself around the upper part of the anchor chain and at some time at high water it had done what it was supposed to do, trip the anchor.

Donald must have got hold of Tom because he suddenly turned up in his boat, reassuring me the yacht was fine and he would take me to her. Meanwhile in Donald's cottage we had a wee dram and a long interesting chat, and Tom told me of his next adventure. He was going to camp out on Rockall, a tiny island in the Atlantic Ocean 240 miles from the Scottish mainland, and claim it for Great Britain. Tom McClean was an ex-SAS soldier and adventurer, so we were able to chat about our forces experiences.

We discussed exploding bolt guns and he asked if I had ever used one. He was going to attach his wooden shelter to the rock with one, but I think he was going to use rope as well. I told him I had heard of them but never used one. Tom said "You've got the perfect boat for taking me and my kit to Rockall, just think of all the publicity you would get. It would to be good for your yacht charter business."

"I know that" I said, but I knew my navigation was not good enough to find what was basically just a small rock in thousands of square miles of Atlantic Ocean. The cheapest satellite plotter was about five thousand pounds in those days, well above my budget.

I retrieved my yacht and anchored back in the bay, without the trip line of course, got my fuel on board and returned the little boat to the estate. The next day I said my goodbyes and got a lift in the big boat over to the jetty on the other side of the loch.

Tom McClean went on to conquer Rockall. In 1985 he stayed on there for forty days, setting up a new record. I believe that record has since been beaten.

Back on board my yacht I tuned in for the shipping forecast. Oh shit, I thought, it was not good. "There are gales in all areas" they said, and then the BBC weather man said "This is the worst forecast I think I have ever had to read." He went on to say that there was a vigorous low coming in from the west and it was deepening with hurricane storm force twelve expected soon. Well, that was all I needed. I would have to ride it out at anchor in the bay, though with the direction of the wind that was forecast I should be quite sheltered.

It all started with the wind shrieking through the rigging like a banshee. I couldn't see the beach about fifty yards away, but I could hear the waves crashing on the shore like thunder. With one ear glued to the radio, I managed to get through the night. The storm reached its peak in the early hours of the morning and continued with howling winds for most of the day. Why is it storms always seem to strike at night? I asked myself. The bay protected me from the massive swell racing past the entrance to it, and I was thankful for that. I remember thinking that the one truly good feeling I had was that I only had myself to worry about. As soon as conditions had calmed down, I sailed back to base in Loch Etive, but more bad weather was on its way. That aviation fuel I got from Meoble worked very well.

Looking back, I went through many other little adventures to earn a bob or two. On one such occasion I was taking a German television crew out to the Garvellachs or Isles of the Sea. I got the job from a friend in London who rang me up to see if I would do it. I agreed, weather permitting, because it would be wintertime when they wanted to go. At 8 am, I picked them up in Oban on the quayside opposite the Oban Inn. The night before it had snowed and then rained, but before the rain had washed off the snow it had frozen, so I had two inches of solid ice on the decks. They turned up and I could hardly believe it – you would think they were going to the theatre rather than out into the open sea. The director wore a full-length camel coat, white trousers and red and cream coloured spats. Only one of the guys was reasonably dressed for the trip, he had a scarf on. There wasn't a welly between them. On top of this they had masses of equipment and we were going to a place where landing was a problem, especially at low tide.

As the day wore on, the sun made an appearance and the ice released its grip on the deck and slid off in slabs. They were going to interview a chap who was an ex-conservative councillor from a London borough, called Robin Pitt, I had met him before on this island. He was living in a nice little cottage which was used as a bothy, living mainly on rabbits and wild mushrooms, having got the necessary permission from the owner. Robin had decided to become a hermit, live on this remote uninhabited island for a year and write a book about it. On passage they got their cameras out and started interviewing me, and I appeared on German TV, so I was told.

The business of getting these guys and their equipment off the boat had to be seen to be believed. The director, him with the spats, was so nimble on his feet, and how he never went down on his backside I will never know. They had to scramble over huge round green slime-covered boulders carrying their equipment, as it was as far as I could take them in the dinghy. Filming took most of the day and when it was time for them to come aboard the tide was in so that made things a lot easier as I was able to get alongside the small jetty. Back in Oban, the film director asked if we, that is me and the chef Alison, would like to join them for dinner at a restaurant of our choosing, and they poetically wanted crab and lobster on the menu. Well, in those days there weren't many eating out places in Oban, even less in winter time. There was only one supermarket, Lows. What seafood the locals caught went down south or to the continent, and you couldn't get a simple thing like mussels on a menu for love nor money. I used to pick my own from the rocks in Loch Etive. We landed up in a hotel restaurant, but the only seafood they had was frozen crab claws served with chips and chopped carrots, and I could see they were very disappointed. I must say today Oban is quite a different town now with lots of lovely eating places.

My mate Mike and I decided to try our luck at getting a stag for the winter. He was a professional deer stalker and had the appropriate rifle licences and ammunition for the job. We set sail for Grass Point on the Island of Mull with the idea of shooting a stag from the boat in the hope that it would fall into the sea where we could get it onto the aft deck; the terrain was mountainous, so it could be done.

Our plans were scuppered by a force eight gale blowing straight up the Firth of Lorne, so we headed for shelter in Craignure. Ashore we visited the shop. Mike knew the owner, who, after introductions, invited us to come for a dram after he had closed for the evening, and we agreed. It was about 7 am when we set out to go to the shop and standing on the pier was the biggest stag you could imagine, just looking at us, and of course we had to shoo it away as it was too close to habitation to shoot.

Later we met Mike's friend and after an hour or so drinking his finest whisky, the local policeman turned up; he was off duty, so he also started on the drams and we had a party. The owner's wife brought in some food and we had a merry old time. When it was time to get back to the boat the policeman walked with us to the pier near where his house was and walked to the end of the pier to see us safely on board. We had a group hug, as you do when you're pissed. His wife was looking at us from the house and could only see our silhouette. She thought we were attacking him and called the main police station in Tobermory, we later learnt.

Next day we invited the store owner and the young Laird of Torosay, who happened to be in the shop at the time and who Mike knew well, to drinks on board the yacht in Loch Spelve, together with a feast of fresh scallops cooked in white wine. Only problem was we didn't have any scallops, so Mike would have to dive for some, and he had been steadily drinking whisky most of the day.

I anchored in the mouth of Loch Spelve and he got his diving gear on. I said "Are you sure you want to do this?"

"No problem" he replied, taking another drink then passing his glass of whisky to me. "Hold that, won't be long". He could jump in from the yacht but couldn't get back on board, so I launched the dinghy to follow him and get him back. He jumped in and within a couple of minutes he was up again.

"What's wrong?" I said.

"I've put an empty air bottle on," he puffed and spluttered out. We changed the bottle and down he went again. His air bubbles exploded at the surface with the strongest smell of alcohol and I was quite worried, but he managed to get a full bag of large scallops and I got him back on board with the aid of the dinghy. We sailed to the arranged meeting place in the east end of Loch Spelve and dropped anchor, Mike sautéed the scallops in butter and white wine and I used the dinghy to get our guests from the jetty to the yacht. We had a fantastic time and it was good for our cred, though I must say we never did get our stag.

I was finding it getting harder to get through winter each year, so it was time to think it out again. I was contemplating putting my beautiful yacht up for sail, but first I tried my hand at mussel farming in Loch Etive. To finance this venture I had a silent partner friend John Kengon, a Dutchman, who came up with a small amount of cash just to get it started. I also contributed a small amount of cash and I did all the work, as well as buying the rope and a steel work boat. I got the relevant permission from the Crown Estate Office in Edinburgh to set up a mussel farm in a remote part of the loch. It was extremely hard work getting all the ropes in position; I calculated that I had the equivalent of six miles of rope stretched across the bay, held in place by chain where the rope would have gone over the rocks to save them from chafing, while large plastic drums were used to hold the rope up at intervals.

After about a year I estimated I had thirty tons of mussels hanging on the ropes, and the floats were just under the water with the weight of them. All I had to do now was wait for the mussels to get to a marketable size, about 45mm. I checked their progress once or twice a month just to make sure they were all right and to scare off any diving birds.

When the time came for harvesting, I got an almighty shock as I approached the site. I could see all the floats blowing in the wind and there were no mussels on the ropes; they were all on the seabed and covered with starfish. Two years and a hell of a lot of hard work wasted. The main problem was diving ducks, goldeneye and eider ducks, eating mussels off the ropes. It wasn't the amount they eat that was the problem, as they didn't eat that many, it was the amount they dislodged from the ropes as they grabbed and scrambled up and down the rope. Most of the mussels were clobbered by their webbed feet, and large clusters of mussels were knocked off every time they dived for them. Mussels grown on ropes don't have such a strong byssus thread as mussels attached to rocks near the shore, so they fall off very easily as they cluster together.

Starfish are another predator of mussels, and the way they eat them is like something out of a horror film. They cover the mussel, or any other shellfish for that matter, and by hydraulic pressure gradually prise the shell open slightly, then inject their stomach parts, rich in special enzymes, into the shellfish. Its contents are liquefied into a kind of soup available for absorption and the starfish then sucks it all back again, leaving an empty shell. I have actually watched a scallop being devoured in this way. I decided it was too big a gamble for me each year, so I got out of the mussel business and it was taken over by someone else.

Eventually I sold the *Hebridean*, my lovely yacht. A guy from Sweden bought it and he wanted me to sail it to Sweden for him. Unfortunately I had other irons in the fire and was committed elsewhere, but I did sail it up to the Caledonian Canal for him. His crew seemed capable, so he was OK.

Chapter 16

Going overboard

~~~~

My mate Mike introduced me to scallop diving, which was a complete change of direction for me. I worked on his boat for a while, getting to know the ropes and learning basic diving skills, and once I realised this was for me, I bought myself a full set of diving gear. I carried on working on my mate's boat for quite a while, and we also did odd jobs such as cleaning mussels and barnacles from under fish farm salmon cages. It was well paid but it was a filthy job, because at the end of the day we were covered from head to toe in fish lice and all kinds of marine creepies. The only way to get rid of them was to leave our dive suits in the sun to dry and brush them off.

One day Mike didn't turn up at the boat yard for a day's diving, so I went to his flat only to find him pissed out of his brain on gin. "Well I guess it's a day off then," I said and ate one of my sandwiches. I then went back home, as he was hard going when he had a drink in him, bless him. Later that night, about eleven o'clock, I got a phone call from a nurse in a Glasgow hospital intensive care unit telling me they had found my phone number in his wallet and wanted to know if I was a family member. "No, I'm his mate" I said. I got the details as to where he was and why he was there – she said he had broken his back in an accident.

I visited Mike in hospital and he gave me the lowdown on what had happened. He had gone out looking for more drink and a bit of company and met a group of lowlifes. They got into an argument and pushed him off a road bridge over a small river in Oban, and he landed on a huge boulder. I was talking to one of the nurses and she said he wouldn't walk again. It was a terrible blow for him, me and all his mates.

With Mike's life-changing injuries it was going to be a long road back, and life would not be the same again for him. I started working as a scallop diver on a boat Mike and I had caulked a couple of years previously when it was owned by a guy called Liam, who had lived on it with his wife. It was a sinking boat then and after all those years it was still a sinking boat. Every morning we had to wade through at least a foot of water just to get into the wheelhouse. At least I was earning money, but not enough. The paperwork was non-existent and it was difficult to know who had earned what and how much. I think I stood it for a couple of months, give or take a week or two, and that was sufficient. In Oban one night I was having a drink in a pub when I met the actual owner of the boat who had bought it from Liam. He told me the boat was not earning him any money and the guys running it didn't seem to bother too much about paying him.

"I'm trying to sell it," he said.

"How much?" I asked.

"I was thinking about three thousand."

"What! The boat's a sinker and it's only a matter of time before it's on the seabed," I pointed out to him.

"I have put a hell of a lot of work in that there boat."

"I know, but it's still a sinker" I said and offered him fifteen hundred. We haggled for some time and I eventually got it for that price. I really think he was genuinely fed up with it constantly costing him money.

I now owned a clapped-out sinking boat. There was quite a history to this old boat as I found out later. It had been a lifeboat from a cruise ship at some time in its past and was found adrift in the north Irish sea. It was American built using Oregon pine planks on an oak frame, there were two-inch thick wooden built-in teak seats all around the deck and it had been acquired by a gentleman in Oban many years before who had put in a new BMC diesel engine with a commodore marinization modification fitted. I have no idea what engine was in before that. The boat was hauled out at Gallanach, where I worked on her to get the hull watertight, and made improvements to the engine such as injector filters, new engine mounts and so on. Because the boat was on dry land I had the opportunity to replace some of the ribs and one of the beams supporting the gunwale.

I applied for a fishing licence and the coastguard came and inspected the work I had done. Then I had to think of a name for the boat. I tried at least a dozen, all of which were rejected by the licensing authority on the grounds that they were already in use. I had been mushrooming the day before and found a load of chanterelle mushrooms, and I wondered what would happen if I submitted the name 'Chanterelle' to the licensing office. Well I did so, and it was accepted. I received my licence just in the nick of time, as the fisheries stopped issuing them and you really had to jump through hoops to get one after that.

So now I was legal. I think I was probably only the second licensed and registered scallop diving boat around Oban waters at that time. I was given a unique boat number which had to be painted on the boat's hull and on the roof of the wheelhouse and a registration number which had to be carved into the boat's main beam. The relaunched boat was a real novelty, as we did not have to pump water out all the time and best of all, we had dry decks to walk on.

I got an old mate, Brian, to be the boatman for me when I was diving by myself; he was a retired chap and was happier to be out doing something than being stuck at home. I paid him one percent of my catch on the sale of it, so the more I earned the more he did. Scallop diving is a very dangerous profession. It's lonely and scary, and you never know what you are going to find down there. You have to break some of the rules, especially if you want to make a living at it. You're down a hundred plus feet on your own with no buddy, and it's hauntingly dark with no colour, as everything at that depth is grey.

We carried on in a small cottage industry way with me finding the best paying markets to sell to. Sometimes on our way home when passing through Oban, I would take a small bag of scallops into the fish and chip shop and swap them for two fish suppers, as they were better than currency in those days. Before long I had other divers asking if they could work on my boat. One of the guys was probably the best scallop diver on the west coast, I was told by other divers, and he proved to be just that, the best. When I had three divers on board, my mate the boatman had to go, as there wasn't enough room for us all. The scallops we were catching filled the decks, and we were earning good money.

I set up a system whereby every diver knew how much he had earned each day. A log book recorded when a diver went down and when he surfaced, his clams were counted and graded extra-large, large, medium and small. They all had different prices and were all counted and entered in a book in size columns. We dived throughout the winter, and when it was very cold we had to hang net bags of clams over the gunwales into the sea to stop them from freezing. In the summer we did the same to prevent them from cooking in the sun. After a couple of years I had one of the most successful commercial clam diving boats in the area, doing thousands of dives a year and attracting the best divers.

Mike had been housed in a special little bungalow for paraplegics. He was able to walk with a stick for very short distances and had plenty of mates visiting him, myself included, and that made him feel happy and wanted. Mike and I carried on having our Christmas office parties at his little house for many years to follow, and it became a sort of tradition.

Making a living in this sort of profession was not easy, as you were so dependent on the weather; the visibility under the sea and gear failure all took their toll. Also, the scallop dredgers played an agonising part in our livelihood by devastating the seabed, killing everything in sight and affecting the underwater visibility for miles around. If you were not gathering scallops, you were not earning money, simple as that. OK, we earned good money, but taken on average, it wasn't that good. One week we might earn well, the next week we couldn't get out because of inclement weather conditions which could be bad for a week or even two.

Having said that there were moments of wonder, especially in the natural world, that never failed to amaze me. One day I was diving north of Inish Island in the Firth of Lorne, a relatively shallow dive of about sixty feet. I was approaching the seabed diving head-first when something waving from side to side just above the muddy seabed caught my eye. It was the discarded stinging tentacles of a lion's mane jellyfish, and attracted to this movement were a dozen or so very small fish. As I got closer to see what was attempting to catch these little fish, a small crab suddenly scurried out of the mud and scampered off, taking the tentacles with it. Now I got to thinking, how does a crab know that these tentacles sting and paralyse fish if they happen to touch them? The crab was unaffected by the stinging cells itself. There had to be an intelligence there, as he was just a wee crab and had not been around long enough to know these things, or so you would think.

Once, diving off the Black Isles, there were only two of us, it was the last dive of the day and I made a very silly mistake. I did my usual fall in backwards off the gunwale and descended to about ten feet, then started to pressurise the dive suit to prevent myself being crushed by the water pressure. I pressed the button and all I got was water flooding in. Oh shit, this is not good, I told myself, I had to go all the way to the seabed eighty feet down and was being crushed by my own dive suit. On the seabed I could hardly move. I had not connected my suit inflation valve and it was impossible to reach and connect it, and even if I could move, I would still be unable to connect it. Got to think this one out, I thought. Now I did have my trusty scallop collecting bag, a net bag with a large opening reinforced by a piece of plastic pipe bent into a ring to hold it open, which was then attached to an inverted plastic container with a hole cut in it near the handle. The idea was to put just enough air in it to lift the bag of clams off the seabed. When you have a full bag, you blow more air in and send it to the surface, where the guy in the boat lifts it aboard.

This then was to be my lifeline back to the surface. I managed to get the container close enough to my mouthpiece to be able to blow air into it, and gradually it started to lift me. I was a bit worried the container wouldn't be big enough to hold the amount of air needed to lift my weight. If this didn't work, I would have to take off my backpack and connect it that way, but this would have been extremely difficult seeing how compressed I was. I had to hold on tight, as if I lost my grip this thing would rocket to the surface and I could become crab meat. I did ascend quite quickly, and because I hadn't been down very long, I hadn't absorbed enough nitrogen in my blood for it to be a problem and give me the bends. Back on board, I connected up my suit and dived in again.

When I got home that night and went for a shower, my whole body was covered in what can only be described as massive love bites where the rubber dive suit had squeezed my flesh, long red-blue bruises the length of my body. "Wow, what's that?" my partner gasped.

"That was one hell of a woman," I said jokingly.

After that experience I made sure I never did it again. I checked everything twice and bought an expensive life jacket with its own inflating system.

Diving near the Bono Rock in the Firth of Lorne I had two divers on board, one an ex-navy diver and the other guy not so experienced. It was spring tides and the tidal flow around these waters are tremendous, to say the least. Sometimes a steady flow can be an advantage, but you need to use a marker buoy so you can be followed by the guy on the boat. These guys didn't want a marker as it can be a drag with such a long rope attached, and they thought they could get some shelter from the tide around the back of the rock outcrop.

So, in they went, and I entered their down time in the logbook. I must say I wasn't happy about the choice of location, but it was what they wanted. Divers do have a certain say as to where they want to dive, and I respected that. It was impossible to follow their air bubbles, as it was too choppy and the tide was running so fast. When you're diving in fast-flowing water and you are descending, there is no indication that you are moving because everything is travelling at the same speed as you, jellyfish or plankton are just hanging there, but as soon as you can see the bottom you realise how fast you are really travelling over the seabed, it's a simplified case of Einstein's theory of relativity.

Their estimated return to surface time had expired and still no sign of them. I was getting worried and scoured the area, nothing. It was now very serious and I picked up the radio handset, selected channel sixteen, that's the international distress channel, and was just about to call Oban coastguard when I saw a fast boat speeding towards me. I recognised the boat and knew the skipper, who was a dive boat skipper but just for visiting sport divers, and he had my two divers on board. I was so relieved, but still gave them a good bollocking. They had been washed away by the tide before they could even reach the seabed. One of them had jettisoned his weight belt to get to the surface, but such was the strength of the tidal stream it had swept them out of the dive area completely. There was a bit of arguing as to whose fault it was, but we got over it.

Most mornings, as we were about to set off on a day's diving trip, the guy who owned the boatyard, old Ted a retired Glaswegian shipyard worker, would come out of his little house overlooking the Sound of Kerrera and shout down at us, "Don't forget lads, if you're alive, you're a millionaire," in a strong Glaswegian accent.

I suppose we were among some of the last real hunter-gatherers, because that's what we did. Quite often, if you came across a part of the seabed with a generous scattering of scallops, it was easy to become greedy. You filled your main bag, the one attached to your float container, and sent it up, but inside the container there was another bag which you took out and this allowed you to carry on gathering. When this one was full there was no way of sending it up, so you had to carry it with you on your ascent. Now this was extremely dangerous, because you had been down so long you had to come up slowly, but because of the extra weight you were carrying, more air had to be put into your dive suit, so if by accident you dropped the bag you would shoot up like a rocket and most likely get an air embolism or bend.

Writing this about shooting up to the surface reminds me of a time I had a novice diver on board; he had so wanted to learn about scallop diving that I took him out with me. It was a lovely calm day and we went to a spot where it was shallow, about thirty or forty feet. I got him ready and he had all the latest diving gear including a brand-new life jacket, the very latest. I was quite impressed. He went down OK, no problems, and I was generally tidying up the boat when suddenly I jumped back in fright and astonishment. There, right at the side of the boat, well above the gunwales, was a man standing on water – well, that's what it looked like – with a very white grim face and extra-large eyes. I blinked and he was gone, and there wasn't a sound. Then he was on the surface and shouting his head off. I got him onboard. "What's wrong?"

"Oh, fucking hell man!" he gasped "I put air into my blob [lifting container] from my mouthpiece, but I forgot to put it back in my mouth before I took another breath." He was coughing and spluttering.

"Never take your mouthpiece out, use the expelled air instead," I told him. The first breath of water had shocked him so much he hit and held the button on his life jacket and came up like a Polaris missile. It frightened him so much I think he stopped diving after that. I pointed out to him that he'd missed the boat by inches and if he'd hit it, he would be dead.

One winter my best diver left my boat to work on another scallop diving boat in a different area, so an old mate of mine called Allan from Orkney Island stepped in to take his place. We worked together very well and he did everything by the book when it came to diving. He stuck to his dive computer rigidly, when his computer told him to surface that's exactly what he did, regardless of how many scallops there were around him. We were diving just off Maiden Island near Oban and there was quite a stiff breeze blowing onto the island. It was a shallow dive, about fifty feet, and Allan went in and took his marker buoy with him on about a hundred and twenty feet of rope. With so much rope in such shallow water it just had to get around the prop and it did. With the prop incapacitated, I was going nowhere.

Allan saw the problem and started untangling the rope, but by the time he had it free, it was too late – the boat had gone aground on a rock and the tide was going out fast. To make things worse, I discovered my radio wasn't working, so I waved down a passing fishing boat to call the coastguard for me, which he must have done because the lifeboat came alongside and offered to pull me off. I declined, thinking they would most likely pull the old boat apart under us. They looked at the old boat and agreed with me. It was a very serious situation. This could wreck the boat, as it was pivoting on a pinnacle of rock and leaning over at a perilous angle. The lifeboat stood by all day until the tide eventually turned and refloated the boat off the rock, and when they were satisfied there wasn't any significant damage to the boat and she wasn't taking on water, they wished me good day. I thanked them very much and gave them a full bag of scallops, our entire catch prior to the disaster, and they were over the moon with their gift.

Chapter 17

Island life

~~~

After this I moved out of my base in Loch Etive and bought a tiny cottage on a very small island. There were no cars on the island, so everything had to be brought on by a small ferry boat not much bigger than a rowing boat. Sometimes it can be quite a character-building experience getting across in certain weather conditions with driving rain and everything getting wet through, then carrying everything in wheelbarrows to wherever you want to go. The island was called Easdale, just off the Isle of Seil, and it had a wonderful social community with lots of social events going on throughout the year. This would save me a hell of a lot of travelling each day. This place was surrounded by sea, all good scallop ground, and it had its own little harbour and moorings. The cottages were small, but the one I bought had an extension built at the back, which made a big difference. The walls were about three feet thick, and they needed to be to cope with the violent storms the island suffered from time to time.

Unfortunately the government then put me out of the scallop-diving business overnight. In 1999 scientists had found a much more sensitive way of detecting a potential poison found in shellfish called amnesic shellfish poisoning, generated when there is an algal bloom in the sea. It was a kind of plankton, and it meant we could not sell our scallops for love nor money. The buyer turned up and said he could not take any shellfish because there was a ban on the sale of scallops in this particular area. So that cost me fifteen hundred quid. I had to take the scallops back to the sea and put them back, and many died as they had been out of water too long.

It was a Labour government at the time and they put hundreds of clam divers on the dole, just like that. Now I'm all for being cautious and safe about what is good to eat but as it turned out, we learnt later, you had to eat an awful lot of scallops to be affected in any way, so I was told. I rang the Scottish office to find out what we could and couldn't do, and they said all the procedures weren't in place yet and it would take some time. I also rang a woman who was in a position to answer questions and was responsible for advice and information. I asked her what this poison did, and she told me it could cause short-term memory loss in humans. I said "I get that every night from a bottle of wine," but I got the feeling she wasn't impressed.

I was now living off my savings, but I knew I couldn't keep that up for long, so I went to the unemployment office to see what could be done. The chap behind the counter said he knew all about the problem and was very apologetic, and said all the Isle of Mull divers were affected as well. I was put on emergency payments until we were allowed back to work. It all became extremely complicated. The sea areas were given box numbers, so if your box was clear you could fish and so we did, but when it came to selling the catch it was a fiasco. I sold a lot of scallops to Loch Fyne Oysters over the years but this time it was different. I took my consignment all bagged up and graded, and the chap in the loading bay said "Have you got a microbiology report on these scallops?"

"Er no, but I've got something better," I said.

"Oh yes, and what would that be then?"

"I've got a diver on board my boat who is too mean to bring sandwiches to work so he eats scallops every day and he's as fit as a fiddle. He also remembers exactly how much I owe him."

"I can't accept that, I need a written report to put into the office," he said, and so there was no sale, but I did manage to sell them elsewhere. The whole scenario turned out to be a complete waste of time and money. I believe it's all back to normal now, but I'm not sure.

As for me, I never really fully recovered, or should I say the boat didn't. I was now past retirement age and I think the boat was too. For instance, with just one diver on board and steaming out to the fishing ground one morning the engine stopped dead and it would not even turn over. I got a tow back into the harbour and found the engine sump had rusted through. This was not the original sump but a homemade mild steel one that had come with the engine. It was an engine I had bought to replace my old engine that had been fitted in a Land Rover, hence the modified steel sump to allow it to fit. I gathered from the guy who sold me the engine that it wasn't very successful in the Land Rover as it couldn't go faster than about twenty-five miles per hour. Being constantly wet from the bilges, the mild steel sump had rusted so thin from constant sea water splashes that the pressure of the oil blew a hole through the bottom of the sump releasing all the oil, so the engine seized solid. I got the boat into the little harbour on the island and during repairs I had the engine on a scaffold platform so I could get to work on it – of course it was much higher than its normal position.

On stripping it down I found the pistons were, as expected, seized solid, along with the big ends, so it was a complete rebuild job. It was moored against the harbour wall and I was getting on well with the repairs but on a very low tide, she was dried out on the seabed when some time in the night, the aft mooring stanchion snapped. The boat rolled over and the engine fell onto the gunwale, pinning the boat down. In the morning when I discovered it, the tide had turned and it was coming into the harbour pretty quickly. There was nothing I could do but watch the sea flood the boat. I managed to get all the electronic equipment off, so that saved quite a replacement expense.

So now I had a sunken boat, and that meant not only the engine to repair but all the electrical wiring to replace. Over the coming days, the good people of Easdale Island helped me get the engine off the boat with an old dumper truck and with the aid of a hired water pump, I got the boat floating again. It was a long hard road getting the boat and engine back to normal, in fact I practically rebuilt her. When I did get the *Chanterelle* shipshape, I had a boat launching party with boxes of wine, nibbles and a gazebo with tables and goodies laid out.

Everyone was invited. The ladies wore their best hats and there was a lone piper on high ground playing a lovely tune which certainly gave the whole occasion some good old-fashioned atmosphere. The whole island turned out with lots of folks, some of whom I didn't even know. Someone had put up bunting and we all had a fantastic time. Breaking the bottle of champagne (well cava actually) over the bow was more difficult than we thought it was going to be, although when a mate and I had tested the launch procedure earlier it had worked very well with ordinary wine bottles. Several attempts were made, but in the end I abandoned the sliding-down-a-rope method and resorted to smashing it over the anchor on the bow. Those champagne bottles are thicker and tougher than you think and twice as thick as an ordinary wine bottle.

A friend who lived on the island had a fishing boat complete with lobster/crab pots and a hydraulic hauler for lifting the pots. He allowed me to use the boat whenever I wanted, as he worked abroad for some oil company and was away most of the time. I put the pots down mainly for table food such as crab and lobster, but we often caught other creatures like octopus and fish, and one day we landed a real monster. Curled up inside a pot was a six-foot conger eel, black as the night. I opened the door of the pot and it shot out onto the deck slithering all over the place, bouncing off the side decks and snapping at anything. It was really bad tempered and they have a very nasty poisonous bite. I pushed it to the side of the boat with a deck brush, hoping to get it through the scuppers, but it was so slippery that each time the boat rocked with the waves, it slid back towards our feet – it must have looked like we were doing a highland fling trying to get out of its way. Eventually I got it off the deck and back into the sea through the scuppers.

On another occasion I hauled in a pot containing a thumping great crawfish – they are like a lobster but without the big claws and quite spiky. Smaller ones fetch a good price and the really big ones are mainly used as a centrepiece for buffet tables at weddings in posh hotels and the like. There were no large functions happening, so I thought I would keep it until there was one. I kept it in a mesh cage in the harbour in about two foot of water, fed it fish and it was doing quite well. After a couple of weeks, it started to go green – they are normally orange colour, not like a lobster, which is blue and goes orange only after being cooked. The green colour was a result of algae growing on him because he was in shallow water and I was beginning to feel sorry for him. Besides, I couldn't sell a green crawfish. I told Annabel I'd dreamt about the crawfish the previous night and he was calling out to me for help as he had a family, so the very next day we took Mr Green, as we now called him, out in the boat to a secret place where he would be safe from other fishermen and divers and let him go free.

During my stay on the island I bought a second-hand aluminium army assault craft complete with an outboard engine. It was fantastic at carrying heavy loads, so I used it to move people and their belongings on and off the island, also theatre groups, their stage, scenery and equipment to the village hall where they would be performing, all for a small fee of course.

I transported just about everything in that assault craft over the years, but one of the saddest trips was taking the ashes of a beautiful young woman who had died far too young. She had wanted her ashes to be scattered on the waters of the Firth of Lorne. In the boat was a priest who read the sermon, members of her family and her young husband. I had known her, as she had sometimes stayed with the people next door to me on the island. When I saw her ashes slowly sink beneath the waves, I could hardly bear it, she was so young.

On Easdale Island, they have the world stone skimming championships every year. It's a fantastic event with up to a thousand people attending, a lot of folk on such a small island. I tried skimming once but it was a flop – don't get me wrong, I can skim very well, but as soon as I get in that quarry with all the people watching me, it's a different ball game. Annabel and I ran the BBQ for this event and did so for seventeen years. We were always thanked at the prize giving but they always referred to us as Sam 'n Ella! (salmonella). They were only joking of course. It was hard work but great fun, and we met lots of nice people over the years.

One day a massive storm hit the island. Of course Easdale gets lots of storms, but I remember this one in particular because it destroyed my car and Annabel's car at the same time. There aren't any cars on the island, so we had to park them on the Isle of Seil, which is quite large and is attached to the mainland by a beautiful stone humpback bridge called the Bridge over the Atlantic. We had parked our cars behind a heavy stone wall. Annabel said to me "Do you think the cars will be all right behind this wall?" and I said "Of course, just look at the size of those boulders, we'll be fine."

We had warning of this pending storm so we were prepared, and we went back to the island to batten down anything that could be blown away. When the storm arrived, it brought with it a huge tide. Some of the cottages were flooded and if it had come another three feet we too would have been flooded. It was about two days before we could get off the island. We did have word from Seil that our cars might be damaged, but when we got over to inspect them, they were basically a write-off. Those big boulders that should have protected the cars were now on top of Annabel's car. Her windscreen was smashed in, and the car was full of salt water. My car had been blown backwards into another car and was badly dented from flying rocks. Annabel's car was much more damaged than mine, but the amazing thing was that hers started first time. We both had to get new cars much sooner than I had expected.

One of the jobs I did each spring was taking a hermit back to his little island – well, it was more like a chunk of rock with grass on it but nevertheless it was a beautiful island. It was the Isle of Inish in the Firth of Lorne, remote and uninhabited, and quite hard to get onto as it had a sheer rock face up from the sea. He lived in a cave on there for the summer months and in winter he would live in a very small cottage on Easdale Island where he spent most of his time collecting food items, non-perishable goods, mostly in tins in preparation for his summer on his island. Getting them onto the island was extremely difficult, but it meant he could live in his cave throughout the summer. He was a great guy, and I got on very well with him. I ferried him on and off the island for about twelve years. He had all the characteristics of what you would expect a hermit to look like, a hunchback and just one big tooth, and a spinal deformity which was a result of polio as a child.

Once he was on his island he did not want anyone to visit him. He made that quite clear when I asked him if I should come and see how he was getting on, because all I got from him was "No, see you in November" (that was when he came back to his tiny cottage on Easdale). Yes, he did own the island lock, stock and barrel.

My job in the spring was to load all his provisions, and there were a lot of them, onto my boat. I had to load him on as well, as he was not very good on his feet. Getting him onto his island was a true work of art, and each time was different. One time I remember it was low water and the rocks were covered in seaweed, so it was very difficult even for me and my helper. I wanted to call it off and wait for a better time but no, he wouldn't have it, so we had to think how to get him on. We tied the boat as tight as we could to the rocks so there wouldn't be any movement and I got a rope around his waist. The idea was for him to crawl up the rocks whist I held him securely with the rope. He started off quite well and got onto the rocks. I shouted to him to start crawling and he did, but then he suddenly rolled over onto his back, which put all his weight onto the rope I was holding. The rope slid up his body and tightened under his armpits. He cried out "Oh no, no, let me go!"

"I can't let you go, you silly bugger!"

He shouted "I would sooner drown than hang!"

"Well I'm not going to let you, OK?"

My helper Jason Rockley, my great nephew, who was there on a camping holiday, and I pulled him up the rocks on his backside till he was on level grassy ground. He was a dead weight, and he was cut and bruised, but happy to be home. It then took him forty-five minutes to get to his cave, about fifty yards away, I must say I was rather worried about how much his health had declined from the previous year. We then humped all his heavy boxes full of tinned food up the hill to his cave dwelling. Throughout all his difficulties he never once let go of a little leather bag he was carrying, and I jokingly said to him once "Is that money you're carrying in that bag?" and he said "Oh no, no!" and gave me a flash of his big tooth. Well whatever that bag contained, it was very important to him.

Getting him off the island was just as difficult as getting him on. It would be the onset of winter, so strong winds and savage tides all added to the problem, and usually there would be only a small window in which to do it. All his belongings would be in the boat ready to go. After a couple of runs up the hill to tell him the wind was getting up and the boat was getting damaged on the rocks he would finally leave the cave entrance, then mumble something to himself and go back to see if he had locked the door to his cave. This would go on for some time. If anyone actually wanted to get into his cave, they could just lift the door and the frame, which was rotten, off the rock, but I never told him that.

On one occasion I heard him having a full-blown conversation with himself. You would have sworn there were two people chatting away, but we loved him for all that. Truth is he did not want to leave. The cave had a sort of door made from an assortment of wooden planks, and there was a window but you couldn't see through it. He had built all this when he was younger. A massive rock about thirty tons in weight had slipped down the rockface, almost blocking out the window, and another much bigger one was hanging up there ready to fall. If it did it would block off the cave entrance and entomb him, but it never worried him in the slightest.

It was a very sad time when the doctors told him he was not well enough to go onto his beautiful little island again. He spent quite some time in hospital and a few years later he died. I reflect that on better times when he could get about the island more easily, he also had a nice little vegetable garden in a more sheltered spot. Sailing round and scallop diving near the island shore, we sometimes caught sight of him having a bath in the sea naked, not an altogether pretty sight. I wondered how he managed to get down to the sea, the rockface being so sheer, but later I discovered that there was a hidden gully in the rock running down to his bathing area.

I remember getting a letter from him; it was so amazing I've still got it somewhere. It was getting near the time when he was due to come off the island. He had somehow managed to attract a party of canoeists, and one of them must have climbed up the rocks to take the letter from him. The envelope said 'To Annabel who works in the Puffer,' and that was it, but she got it anyway. The letter read 'Generator stopped working, could not contact Clyde coastguard, Dave come'. Normally he contacted the coastguard and they contacted me by phone and we would set a time for him to come off.

Sometimes dolphins and even killer whales would visit the waters around Easdale Island and it never failed to bring excitement, especially to the children who had to cross the Easdale Sound to get to school each morning. They were always in a playful mood jumping high out of the sea showing off to the kids, and many times they had their own young with them.

I spent many wonderful years on Easdale Island with too many memories to record. The Scottish people are some of the kindest and friendliest folk I have ever met.

Chapter 18

Into the woods

~~~~~

Annabel and I obtained a small plot of land on the mainland, a quarter of an acre of woodland, which had beautiful views of the mountains but was basically a massive patch of bracken standing six feet tall and covering the whole site. I can tell you now it took eleven years to get rid of it without using chemicals.

I wanted to build a wooden house, and studied all the options. It needed to be strong, well insulated and a reasonable price. There were a lot to choose from, but most of them were nothing more than sheds, some of which were an insult to your intelligence. Local timber was very expensive and not quite what I was looking for.

My search took me to a firm in Dundee on the east coast of Scotland. The director was a structural engineer with a beautiful Latvian wife who was a very active member of the building firm, and they knew exactly what they were talking about. We discussed the U value of of the timber and other insulation, and they supplied fantastic log houses machined in Latvia from slow-grown Baltic pine which slotted together to make windproof joints whilst keeping its insulation properties. They showed me samples of the logs, which were substantial for building a log house, just what I was looking for.

We negotiated a price and all the components of the house had to be shipped from Latvia. I was to do the foundations, pay for the slate covering of the roof and so on. I had renovated four houses in the past, two of them from uninhabitable condition to lovely dwellings, but I had never built one from scratch. I finally got planning consent and a building warrant, having jumped through all the hoops and ticked all the boxes, and once they were out of the way things started to happen pretty quickly.

The day came when I got a phone call telling me the first lorry was almost at the village. We had to race down our single-track road to tell the driver to stop, as he wouldn't be able to get up our road because his vehicle was too big. This meant waiting in a layby, then leaping out in front of a huge articulated lorry with Russian symbols on the front and wildly waving it down into the layby. The lorry driver was Russian and could not understand a word of English, but with a lot of gesturing, pointing and grimacing, we got him to do what had to be done. I hired someone to organise guys with forklift trucks who could unload the logs into the layby. He also carted all the logs and finishing timbers up to the site on a large trailer, which was a tremendous help. There were five or six lorries in all, I can't remember exactly, but amazingly we found four people in this small village of Kilchrenan who spoke fluent Russian.

I was seventy when I built this log house. I call it a house because it has four bedrooms and is big, nothing like the small log cabins your mind might conjure up when I say my house is made of logs. It rained almost every day right through the building process. Once all the logs were in place it looked enormous. The downstairs rooms were nine feet high and the supporting timbers throughout the house were huge. I thought it was over-engineered, but then I remembered where this house came from, which is a country where they can have up to fifteen feet of snow on the roof in winter.

As the build progressed and before the doors and floor were completed, I put in all the electric cables and central heating pipes. When the guys left, eight weeks to the day from when they arrived, it was now up to me to get the house habitable. I got local roofers to slate the roof and they made a good job of it. I built all the internal walls, partitioning off the bedrooms, ensuite bathroom, all the plumbing including eleven radiators throughout the house all running off a large cast iron wood burning stove, all the electrics, everything. I never had any help apart from Annabel, who did an enormous amount. It was about two years before I got the house properly finished and I can still find lots of things to do.

At the age of seventy-six, I bought myself some mountain climbing gear. There was a big sycamore tree threatening the workshop I had built, and the only way I thought I could deal with it was to take it down from the top, hence the climbing gear. I spent a lot of time researching and then bought the equipment I needed to do the job. It was easier said than done. I got part of it down, but that was as far as I could go, so I admitted defeat with the climbing gear, although it came in handy when I built the garage and elevated summerhouse. One windless day I cut the sycamore tree down with a chainsaw. It fell exactly where I planned it to fall, but it was a bit scary all the same.

My climbing gear came in handy for something else though. On Easdale Island, between Annabel's and her neighbour's cottage, was an enormous pine tree that was threatening to fall and cause considerable damage. Whenever there was a gale its roots could be seen moving up and down. It was getting very unstable and so it had to come down. Problem was nobody would do the job because of its proximity to the cottages' power lines and phone cables. Because this was a disaster waiting to happen, I decided to do the job myself even though there were so few trees on the island and it seemed a shame to cut it down. It was a weekend, so there were quite a few people about. I cut the large branches off as I progressed up the tree, each time leaving enough branch to climb onto, and some of the really big ones I lowered down by rope so I could control their fall. When I was at the stage where I was about to take the top off, I kind of lost my nerve, especially as there were people standing around in groups watching. I thought "I'm not entertaining them with what could be a potential disaster," so I came down to think about it. I must say I wasn't very confident cutting the tree top off, it was so big.

It was about eight o'clock in the evening, so I sat down, had four cans of lager and thought about it. Suddenly I said "Damn it, I'm going to do it." Chemically supercharged with alcohol, up the tree I went armed with a bow saw. Hooded crows had built a nest there, and over many years it had got bigger and thicker with each year, so I had to break my way through it to get to the main trunk, and it was lathered in creepy crawlies. I tied myself on, tightened my safety helmet and cut through the top. It fell into the garden area, taking with it the lean-to, which was no problem as it was due to be demolished. It had fallen just where I had wanted it too and nobody was more surprised than I was. Next day locals thought Annabel had got professionals from the mainland to do it. She said "No, it was only Dave".

The first winter in the house proper I noticed footprints in the snow all around the house – cat prints. I had set some mouse traps around the place, which had all disappeared, and I suspected it was a cat taking them off to eat the contents. Years later I found all the traps under a pile of old wood. There were two cats in the area, one we called Ringo because of the lovely rings on her tail, the other we called Misty as she was all grey with long fur and you could not get anywhere near this cat ever. It took about three years to really get to know Ringo, and she has now adopted us. She is a wonderful cat and a deadly hunter, but unfortunately she also catches red squirrels and eats them, tail and all. She is now called Quazmanix. I can't think why, the name just came out of the top of my head, and she has trained us to look after her. This cat follows us wherever we go and she is very protective if we go into dark woodland – it's easy to see that she is guarding us. She has perfect Scottish wildcat markings apart from a little too much white on her face and paws, so she is classed as a hybrid Scottish wildcat by the Scottish Wildcat Association.

I went on to build a big workshop using some logs and timber left over from the main house. This was quite a challenge, which I tackled by myself, and the only thing I didn't do was putting the slates on the roof. A month later I found there was a leak on the upstairs ceiling around the skylight which was to do with the flashing not being long enough under the slates, so I fixed it myself. My next job was building the garage, followed a few years later at the age of seventy-nine by a summer house using heavy pine tree trunks which had been blown down in the forest. It's an elevated construction with part of it built on log stilts. Both the garage and summerhouse have slate roofs which I put on myself with the aid of my climbing gear. I can look out over the surrounding woodland and see what wildlife is about. There are three type of deer living here red, roe, and sika, and they all come into the garden to feed on whatever they can get their teeth into, so we have to protect everything we grow with fencing.

I have just had my eightieth birthday party, in the village hall on Easdale Island, and storm force winds the day before meant the ferry couldn't run. This kept some distant friends of mine from attending, but it didn't deter my daughter Corrine and my eighty-seven-year-old brother Rex, his son Ian and Ian's girlfriend, who came up from Nottingham the day before the storm. It was a really fantastic party and it was so nice to see so many friends and acquaintances gathered in one place. Annabel organised it all, with the help of other Island friends. Thank you all from the bottom of my heart.

I'm intending to restore a beautiful wooden boat that has been lying on the shores of Loch Awe for about fifteen years. She is in a very sorry state with many of the hull timbers rotted through. It will certainly be an enormous challenge at my age, but it will keep me active and out of mischief. Why this boat? Well she is 92 years old, built by C.H. Breaker at Bowness on Windermere in the Lake District in 1927. I knew this boat in 1982 as she was moored near me on the River Trent when I was fitting out my Snowgoose 37-foot catamaran before I sailed up to Scotland. Originally named *The Lady Rowena*, she had a Morris Eight car engine in her, but she was later sold and shipped to Glasgow, where she was fitted with a peat-fired steam engine and boiler, then launched on Loch Awe, where I met her once again. Now renamed Gertrude Matilda, I honesty couldn't believe my eyes when I saw her, it was quite a remarkable coincidence. This boat really must be following me, so I have to do what I can for this lovely old boat; she really is part of my history.

Well, I'm off now to enjoy a glass of cool lager in the summerhouse, watch the red squirrels scamper across the trees, make sure the deer aren't eating too many of the vegetables, and plan my next adventure.

BV - #0011 - 191119 - C17 - 229/152/16 - PB - 9781861519467